The East Donegal Border Petition

Maynooth Studies in Local History

SERIES EDITOR Michael Potterton

You are reading one of the six volumes in the Maynooth Studies in Local History (MSLH) series for 2023. A benefit of being the editor of this series is the early opportunity to read a very wide variety of bite-sized histories covering events and activities from the magnificent to the outrageous in every nook and cranny of this remarkable island. This year's offerings take us from Bronze Age burials in west Kerry to a three-year dairy war in 1930s east Donegal, via an entrepreneur extraordinaire from late Georgian Cork, a revelatory survey of dire poverty in pre-Famine Westmeath, a century of exclusive terrace-life in colourful Tralee and the complex social networks of a family of Francophile Catholic landed gentry from Kildare. Together, these six studies take us on an astonishing journey on which we encounter smugglers, umbrella makers, lifelike automata, difficult marriage- and education choices, resolute defiance, agrarian violence, rapidly changing religious and political landscapes and a petition to have a region transferred from one nation to another.

These half-a-dozen volumes show how the 'local' focus of a *local history* can range from an individual person (Marsden Haddock) to a family (the Mansfields), a street (Day Place), a village (Portmagee), a county (Donegal and Westmeath) and beyond. The six authors have taken their stories from relative obscurity to centre stage. Denis Casey now joins Terence Dooley as one of only two people to have published three volumes in this series (though they are set to be joined by a third in 2024!).

This year in the Department of History at Maynooth University we are celebrating seventy years of excellence in teaching, research and publication (1953–2023) and we are especially delighted to be relaunching our enormously successful MA in Local History. Theses from this programme have traditionally provided the backbone of the MSLH series and we look forward to another rich crop in the years to come.

Whether you ask Alexa, ChatGPT or Raymond Gillespie, there is no doubting that Local History is valuable and significant. AI has evolved considerably since I grew up on a dairy farm in south Co. Meath and it is sure to play an increasing role in the research, writing and dissemination of local history. As with so many new technologies, of course, the greatest challenge is perhaps going to be maximizing the potential of Artificial Intelligence without compromising the integrity of the results.

Maynooth Studies in Local History: Number 160

The East Donegal Border Petition and the Derry–Donegal Milk War, 1934–8

Samuel Gary Beckton

FOUR COURTS PRESS

Set in 11.5pt on 13.5pt Bembo by
Carrigboy Typesetting Services for
FOUR COURTS PRESS LTD
7 Malpas Street, Dublin 8, Ireland
www.fourcourtspress.ie
and in North America for
FOUR COURTS PRESS
c/o IPG, 814 N Franklin Street, Chicago, IL 60610

© Samuel Gary Beckton and Four Courts Press, 2023

ISBN 978-1-80151-093-6

Printed in Ireland
by SprintPrint, Dublin

Contents

Acknowledgments

I would like to express my gratitude to many people and institutions for assisting me with this work. For their advice on source materials and other favours, I would like to thank Dr Emmet O'Connor, School of Arts and Humanities, Ulster University; Dr Margaret O'Callaghan, School of History, Anthropology, Philosophy and Politics, Queen's University Belfast; Prof. John Lambert, Department of History, University of South Africa; Prof. David Wilson, Department of History, University of Toronto; and Stewart McClean, Project Orange and the Newtowncunningham Community Outreach Project. I would also like to thank John Rankin, grandson of Thomas Boyd Rankin; Marion Bennett, granddaughter of Robert William Glenn; George Fleming, grandson of James Taylor Fleming; and Mary Hamilton, niece of William John Greer Throne, for their help with the photographs in this book. It is a pleasure to thank Nick Wedd at maproom.org for permission to use the image reproduced on the cover.

This work would not have been accomplished without the help of the staff of the following institutions: British Library; National Library of Ireland; National Archives of Ireland; Public Record Office of Northern Ireland; Donegal County Council; Donegal County Library; Library and Archives Canada; Orange Heritage Museum; Donegal County Museum.

Finally, and most importantly, I want to thank my family for their continued encouragement. I dedicate this work to my grandparents, Santina and Wasyl Macyk, who taught me the importance of community and remembrance of one's cultural heritage.

Introduction

During the early twentieth century, Co. Donegal Unionists, primarily Protestant, campaigned against the implementation of Irish Home Rule, and for Ulster to remain in the United Kingdom. In 1912, over 18,000 Donegal Unionists signed the Ulster Covenant and Declaration, later forming five Ulster Volunteer Force (UVF) battalions with 3,360 members, and stood against the local Irish Volunteers who were created following the UVF's establishment to ensure Home Rule was implemented.[1] During the First World War, 8,000 Donegal Protestants and Catholics enlisted in the British military for different reasons. For Unionists it was to prove their loyalty, for Irish Nationalists they followed John Redmond's call to enlist in order to secure Home Rule and defend the small nation of Belgium; while for others it was for employment or a chance to see the world.[2] From December 1914 to December 1915, there were 648 recruits to the British Army from the county. Of these, 177 were members of the UVF, 321 were members of the Irish National Volunteers (the Irish Volunteers that sided with John Redmond), and 150 had unknown backgrounds.[3] Recruitment in the county was poor, regardless of religion. By 1916, there was an estimated 21,400 men of military age in the county that had not yet enlisted. Many farmers tended to be apprehensive of enlisting, choosing to remain at home to reap financial gain due to the boom in demand for agriculture the war had caused.[4] Approximately 1,200 men from the county were reported to have been killed in action.[5] In the 1918 general election, Major Robert Lyon Moore stood as a Unionist candidate for East Donegal, beating Sinn Féin, but not the Irish Parliamentary Party, for the seat.[6] Nevertheless, in the 1920 local elections the rural district councils of Londonderry no. 2 and Strabane no. 2, located in east Donegal, were the only rural councils of which Unionists retained control outside the six counties that became Northern Ireland.[7] These efforts to prove themselves were in vain, however, as Donegal was allocated to Southern Ireland under the Government of Ireland Act

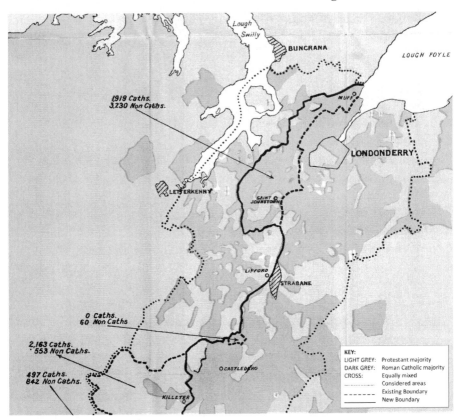

1919 Caths.
3,230 Non Caths.

0 Caths.
60 Non Caths.

2,163 Caths.
553 Non Caths.

497 Caths.
842 Non Caths.

KEY:
LIGHT GREY: Protestant majority
DARK GREY: Roman Catholic majority
CROSS: Equally mixed
.... Considered areas
- - - - - -   Existing Boundary
————————   New Boundary

1. The 1925 Irish Boundary Commission Report demographic justifications for boundary alterations for east Donegal, using the 1911 census (TNA, Report of the commission, CAB 61/161)

1920, while the 1921 Anglo-Irish Treaty solidified the boundary. Appeals to the Ulster Unionist Council (UUC) fell on deaf ears, as they abandoned counties Cavan, Donegal and Monaghan due to their large Catholic populations.[8] Their hopes that the Irish Boundary Commission would rectify this came to nothing as the border remained unchanged.[9]

The Unionist community, though betrayed and abandoned, adapted to their new life in the Irish Free State. The Donegal Unionist Association was reformed into the County Donegal Protestant Registration Association (CDPRA), with 13 of its 36 branches located in north and east Donegal by 1925.[10] The CDPRA changed their chosen designation from Unionism or Loyalism to political

Protestantism instead. Unionists support Ireland's union with Great Britain, while Loyalists, who may not have been in the UK, still identified themselves as British subjects. They felt the Great Britain was their cultural motherland, and advocated for close economic, political and cultural ties with both the UK and the rest of the British Empire.[11] The CDPRA focused on the interests of its community, submitting evidence to the Irish Boundary Committee that Donegal should be included in Northern Ireland, and rallying the Protestant community to elect their own independent candidates for local and general elections to ensure political representation.[12] The association had the support of the local Orange Order, an Irish Protestant fraternity order that was traditional Unionist, and the Grand Orange Lodge of Ireland remained united as a single body despite partition.'[13]

In November 1934, Unionists in east Donegal and the Laggan Valley decided to undertake a new kind of political activism: a petition, called a 'Memorial', detailing their plight and case for east Donegal to be incorporated into Northern Ireland. The Boundary Commission Report, chaired by Justice Richard Feetham, recommended that 31,114 acres of east Donegal be transferred to Northern Ireland based on local demography and economics. This would affect just a fraction of the Protestant community in east Donegal, transferring only a population of 5,209, of which 3,290 were Protestants (fig. 1).[14] This was unknown to east Donegal Unionists; the Boundary Commission's report was not released to the public by the British government until 1 January 1968.[15] The only map that was published concerning the potential recommendations of the Boundary Commission was circulated by the *Morning Post* after someone leaked information to the newspaper, yet even this version suggested parts of east Donegal were to be transferred to Northern Ireland (fig. 2).[16] Donegal's Protestant population declined from 35,516 in 1911 to 27,567 in 1926, and to 23,404 by 1936. This was a significant 34.1 per cent drop, yet east Donegal maintained a large Protestant community (fig. 3).[17]

Despite the uniqueness of this southern Unionist movement, little has been written about this Memorial, which challenges Patrick Buckland's claim that the 'southern Anglo-Irish ... bowed to the political aspirations of the majority of their countrymen'.[18] Both Dennis Kennedy and Uinseann MacEoin wrote a brief history of the Memorial – how many signed the document, its link to de Valera's

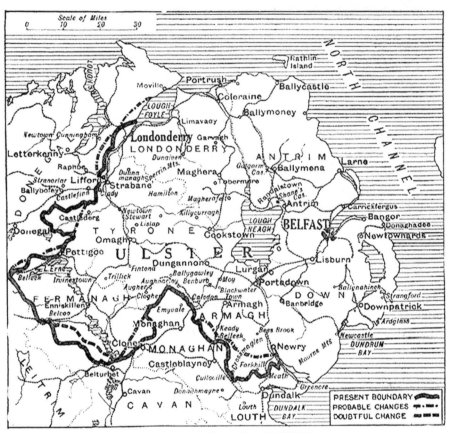

THE BOUNDARY POSITION

2. 'The Boundary Position' (*Morning Post*, 7 Nov. 1925)

economic policies, and the initial reactions of Westminster, Stormont and local authorities in Donegal as they tried to deal with the matter swiftly.[19] However, they did not assess who organized the Memorial or the reaction of the press, except for Kennedy in regards to the *Belfast News-Letter*. Robin Bury does briefly mention the Memorial as a reaction from Donegal farmers during the Economic War, yet he makes two errors. First, he believed the petition had 16,000 signatures, more than double the number the Memorial ever claimed.[20] Second, he claims the source of his information was an MA thesis by John Tunney, 'From ascendancy to alienation: a study of Donegal's

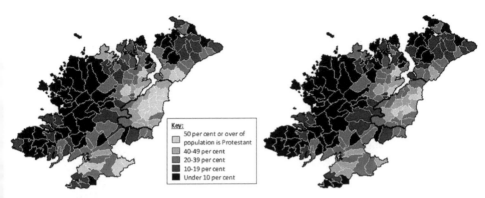

3. Outline of the Laggan Valley, and a comparison of the 1911 and 1936 censuses in the District Electoral Divisions of Co. Donegal (North Eastern Boundary Bureau, *Handbook of the Ulster question* (Dublin, 1923), pp 66–77; Department of Industry and Commerce, *Census of population, 1936, vol. III* (Dublin, 1939), pp 97–100)

Protestant community, 1881–1932'. But this thesis never mentions the Memorial.[21]

David Fitzpatrick and John Tunney show how the Donegal Protestant community in the early post-partition years continued their political involvement in the Free State through the election of their own representatives, such as independent Protestant TD Major James Sproule Myles.[22] Nevertheless, Fitzpatrick does not discuss their relation to the Memorial. The current book follows a more revisionist approach, following the style of Brian Hughes and Conor Morrissey in their essay collection on the history of how southern Irish Loyalists adapted to post-partition Ireland up to 1949.[23] Katherine Magee's contribution to Hughes and Morrissey's work discusses the life of one of these possible Memorialists, Lieutenant-Colonel John George Vaughan Hart. Magee discusses Hart's life as a case study of how partition affected large southern Irish landowners, especially in the border counties, and how they tried to respond to these political changes.[24] As John Bowman explained, Unionists were as 'devotedly attached to the empire as [Irish Nationalists] were to independence', a sentiment that took decades to fade;[25] this conservative devotion to British ideals was deeply rooted in east Donegal, becoming a hotbed of British irredentism.

For Ian d'Alton and Ida Milne, a two-sided process occurred in Ireland, a combination of accommodation and tolerance by the majority Catholic community to the minority Protestant community that needed to find its place in the new state after partition.[26] Joseph Ruane and David Butler reinforced this by discussing the transition of identity for southern Irish Protestants from a British ethnic group to a religious minority in Ireland. Nonetheless, the research focuses on Cork, where inter-religious relations were different to those in Donegal.[27] Terence Dooley's work on Monaghan Protestant history from 1912 to 1926 is a better comparison. North Monaghan and east Donegal had identical experiences from 1912 to 1925 and adapted to partition in similar ways. He criticizes how the majority of works concerning the history of Ulster Unionism are flawed by just giving 'fleeting' references to the Protestants of Cavan, Donegal and Monaghan, focusing on their six-county counterparts, and ignoring their contribution to Unionism because they were left out of Northern Ireland.[28] Another substantial study is Tim Wilson's comparison of community relations within Ulster and Upper Silesia from 1918 to 1922. Irish Free State border Protestants and the German minority in Upper Silesia had similar experiences during the inter-war period. Wilson illustrates how conflict and new boundaries affect perceptions of local culture and identity through reactions by the local populace to these political changes and how forms of irredentism emerge, demographic population shifts, the impact on inter-community relations, and the legacies that remain.[29]

This book is intended to fill the academic gap concerning the history of the east Donegal Memorial. Its primary aims and objectives are, first, to investigate the Memorial's origins, its circumstances, and how it came about. Second, to uncover the instigators of the movement, what their background and motives were, and what role they undertook. Third, to analyse how the campaign developed over time, in particular its reception by politicians and the press within Ireland and the British Empire, and their reactions. Lastly, to evaluate what were the overall successes and failures of the Memorialists. Even if the border remained unaltered, did the Memorial manage to achieve something for the residents of east Donegal?

1. Origins of the Memorial

The Memorial was a reaction to Éamon de Valera's policies after the 1932 general election. Fianna Fáil started the process of cutting the Free State's ties with the UK by abolishing the oath of allegiance, the right of appeal to the Privy Council, and prerogatives of the governor general.[1] The most important change for southern Loyalists was the Irish Free State Citizenship Bill, altering the state's nationality laws from British subjects to Irish citizens.[2] The Statute of Westminster 1931 made these changes legal. To exacerbate matters, an Anglo-Irish trade war, the Economic War, took place from 1932 to 1938, depressing agricultural prices. Its impact was especially felt in the border counties that relied on cross-border trade.[3] These changes became too much for some to bear. The first appeal for help from Donegal Loyalists was in 1933, when a letter was sent to the duke of Abercorn, governor of Northern Ireland, by 'Unionists of the Free State'. They claimed they were ready at any moment to migrate to Northern Ireland if they could sell their properties, asking if they were to be left to fend for themselves 'among the lions'.[4]

Over time, there was an increased stir of local political activism in the county, especially during election periods, which saw an increase in voter turnout. In the 1933 general election, the constituency of Donegal voter turnout increased from 74.1 to 78.5 per cent from the previous election in 1932. Myles topped the poll again to get the first seat with 10,784 votes, instead of the 10,077 votes he received in the previous election.[5] The local election the following year saw an increase in voter turnout as well in the local electoral areas that covered north-east Donegal for the Donegal county council under the single-transferable-vote system. In Buncrana, the turnout increased from 37.3 to nearly 73.4 per cent, and in Letterkenny it increased from 59.4 to 81.1 per cent. The CDPRA candidates polled particularly well in the election, Basil McCrea and Captain William Harnott Wagentreiber came second and third in both the poll and the election of seats in Letterkenny, while Captain John Scott won

the first seat in Buncrana with 1,064 votes on the first count. No
other candidates were elected on the first count in Buncrana, Fine
Gael came second with 680 votes and Fianna Fáil third with 622
votes.[6] This level of political activity by ex-Unionists was similarly
seen in counties Cavan and Monaghan, who were able to elect
their own independent councillors and TDs during this time.[7] This
could be compared to the political activity of the German minority
in Poland during the same period. They were able to elect local
government representatives in the Pomeranian, Poznań and Silesian
Voivodeships.[8] During the 1935 legislature election in Poland, three
German independents were elected as deputies in the Sejm, the lower
house of the Polish parliament.[9] Despite the increased voter turnout,
however, the CDPRA had only one TD out of eight designated seats
for Donegal and five out of 36 seats on the Donegal County Council.
For east Donegal, there were eight seats available in Buncrana and
seven in Letterkenny, but the CDPRA could get only three.[10]
Despite having attained this distinct political identity some Donegal
Protestants began to support Fine Gael, as they felt the new Free
State government was beginning to target them. On 14 June 1934,
an amendment on the Electoral Division (Constituencies) Bill divided
the Dáil's eight-seat Donegal constituency into Donegal East with
four seats and Donegal West with three seats. Daniel McMenamin,
Fine Gael TD for Donegal, was one of the few to strongly oppose the
amendment. He claimed no county had suffered more from partition
than Donegal, and electoral division was morally wrong for it would
disenfranchise 4,000 to 5,000 south Donegal Protestants who would
be unable to elect their own candidate.[11]

  These acts of political activism quickly began to be seen outside
of election periods, with an element of open defiance towards the
local and national government. There were claims an east Donegal
Tenants' Association was established by the tenants of labourer
cottages in Raphoe, St Johnston, Ballindrait, Lifford and Castlefin
with the intention to not pay any rent.[12] Though the names of all
the striking tenants were not announced, these were areas with large
Protestant communities.[13] The strikers believed they were entitled to
50 per cent rent reductions and to have all arrears written off, as had
happened with the land annuities. Tenants in these areas had not paid
rent for the past year, with some going as far as two or more years,

even though the rent for the cottages was claimed to be the cheapest in the whole of the Free State at £1s. 9d. to £2s. 3d. per week. Other areas in the county had defaulters, but with just one or two cases. Only in these east Donegal districts was there a mass organized form of defaulting. This came to light as a representative of the Board of Health in the county, Mr J. Fitzmaurice, appeared at Raphoe District Court on 27 November 1934 to prosecute a number of local labourer tenants to recover the possession of cottages owned by the board.[14]

A few weeks after the 1934 local election, Donegal Orangemen joined their counterparts from the City of Derry/Londonderry, North, Mid and West Tyrone in a Twelfth of July demonstration in Woodend, Strabane. Up to one hundred lodges were present at this parade. There was a speech by the chairman of the demonstration, Revd Thomas Alexander Hickson Moriarty. When he extended a greeting to the Free State Orangemen, it showed he knew a border petition was being planned or else he made a strangely accurate prediction:

> There are, we know, many loyal hearts and true in that distressful country. Nay, more, I am convinced that if they dared but speak, there are countless thousands who, though not members of our Order, and who do not even worship at the same shrine, who are still loyal to the Empire, and who desire to see the whole country united in one holy and loyal bond of Imperial unity. Perhaps that day is not so far off as some people may imagine. We take off our hats to those brave men and women who, against almost overwhelming odds, still strive to keep the old faith, walk in the old paths, and uphold the well-worn flag of liberty.[15]

The Memorial was reported by the press to have possibly emanated from Belfast to safeguard Donegal milk vendors and farmers from the Milk and Milk Products Act 1934, which was passed through the Northern Irish parliament. The act would prevent Free State farmers from trading north of the border unless they were registered, graded and had a licence. This cut Donegal farmers off from their traditional markets in Derry/Londonderry and Strabane.[16] A related possible source of the Memorial, according to the press and the Gardaí, was Unionist traders from the city of Derry/Londonderry affected by tariffs from both sides of the border.[17] Another possible root was a

'Future of Northern Ireland' event on 29 March 1934 at Ballynafeigh
Orange Hall for the St Jude Polling Station and the Ormeau Unionist
Association. Speaker William John Stewart, Westminster MP for
South Belfast, proclaimed:

> I would suggest that we should claim definitely that Donegal
> should be included in Northern Ireland. If the Irish Free State
> say that Ireland is mutilated, we also say that Ulster is mutilated,
> and that if any readjustment is to take place, Donegal at least
> should be returned to us so that our geographical position here
> may be strengthened.[18]

Canvassing for the Memorial began on 5 November and went
on until 13 November in the predominantly Protestant regions of
east Donegal. The Gardaí reported on 7 November that two men
were canvassing in Muff, and suspected that similar activities had
been undertaken in the region from Letterkenny to Ballybofey. By
15 November, the Gardaí reported that signatures were secured in
Carrigans, Muff and Newtowncunningham, but canvassers did not
appear to have gone any further into Laggan Valley. They believed
the Memorialists' activities became restricted after gaining attention
from the local authorities and press.[19] There were press reports the
Memorial had gone across the Laggan Valley, however, and as far as
Letterkenny and Inishowen.[20] The document was reported to have
been widely embraced by the Unionist community, but no Catholics
were approached. Some refused to sign the Memorial for three
reasons: disagreement with its sentiment and aim; fear of retaliation
from Free State authorities or Irish republicans; and lack of faith
in what could be achieved given their experience with the UUC's
'broken Covenant' betrayal.[21]

There is no clear indication of how many were involved in the
Memorial; no names were given and the process itself was handled
with great secrecy to protect their identities and families from
potential harassment or persecution. On 15 November a Garda report
identified eight men who collected signatures for the Memorial.
These were John Orr, Samuel Gallagher and Thomas Boyd Rankin
from Carrigans, and John Wylie, John Rankin, Herbert Stewart,
George Keyes and William Acheson, an agent in the county for

Lieutenant-Colonel Hart (Kilderry), from Muff. Another report on 1 December increased this list again to include James Fleming and Samuel Alexander from St Johnston, John McBeth and Robert McGonagle from Lifford, Alexander Wilson from Carrickmore, and David Rankin from Carrigans. All were known Presbyterian or Church of Ireland Unionists. Due to the secrecy under which the Memorial operated, no members of the Presbyterian, Church of Ireland or Methodist clergy were identified as being involved as they had been during the Ulster Covenant. The fact that the canvassers were primarily farmers demonstrates how desperate the Economic War made them. At this time, 40 per cent of Derry/Londonderry's milk supply came from Donegal, together with other produce.[22]

The Memorial was reported to have been passed from house to house under a veil of the strictest secrecy, with not a single copy to be found in Donegal afterwards, as they were burned. This approach was a double-edged sword for the organizers. Contacting only those believed to be sympathetic and who could be trusted hindered their potential to maximize signatures. Whether this level of secrecy was truly employed remains unclear, but this meticulous approach worked well. Free State authorities never obtained a copy of the Memorial, despite their best efforts, and they were only made aware of it by 7 November, days after canvassing had started. Members of the Special Detective Unit from Dublin were dispatched to Donegal to carry out investigations, but their presence was noticed by journalists, which made the story more interesting for them to report.[23] Most letters and reports of the Garda investigation were classified as state secrets, with both the Department of Justice (*An Roinn Dlí agus Cirt*) and the Department of Local Government and Public Health (*An Roinn Rialtais Áitúiula agus Sláinte Puibli*) particularly being kept informed. While the Gardaí did turn up information in its own investigation, there were moments when the press were ahead of them, particularly the *Derry Journal*. These press developments were often mentioned in their reports, including clippings of the articles, and sometimes inspired them to investigate certain elements. The majority of the Garda reports came from the acting Ard-Cheannphort in Letterkenny, Herbert V. McManus. In his initial report on 7 November he was impressed by the Memorialists, but he felt the Irish government needed to be notified immediately of the 'aggressive and hostile attitude of the non-Catholic and Unionist section of the population in the county and its parent body in the Six Counties'. McManus did appear to have preconceptions concerning the Protestant community, describing the Laggan Valley on 15 November as 'alien in its outlook in every way'. By 5 December, he had a 'non-Catholic Unionist' informer keeping tabs on the movement, and at one point suspected they were conducting their business in Freemason halls, even though the Masonic Order has mixed religious denominations and does not discuss politics, unlike the Orange Order.[24] This confusion and these preconceptions were due to his inexperience of the county's community affairs. He had just transferred to Letterkenny from the Garda Depot in early 1934, after serving two years in Bray, Co. Wicklow.[25] McManus let his opinion of the Memorial investigation and political attitudes be known on 12 December 1934, claiming:

> None of these petitions and suggestions seem to be worthy of serious consideration from a police point of view, but they are illuminating from the point of view of the ultimate national aim in this state.[26]

Due to his suspicions of how serious the Memorial could be, he recommended the Garda commissioner, Eamon Broy, on 7 November to direct enquiries to see if other Unionist petitions were happening in counties Cavan and Monaghan.[27] While there was an element of irredentist desire among southern Unionists to restore their place in the UK, especially in the border counties, no other Unionist petitions took place. The 1925 Boundary Commission recognized that Cavan and Monaghan had few Protestant communities close to the border and had alternative markets in their regions to trade their goods, weakening their case to be transferred. East Donegal was largely an economic hinterland of Strabane and Derry/Londonderry, thus more affected by the Economic War than Cavan or Monaghan. Some areas of Drummully, Mullyash and Churchill in Monaghan were to be transferred to Northern Ireland. But the Boundary Commission Report remained secret and the recommendations were unknown to local residents; the map from the *Morning Post* showed no area of Monaghan was to be ceded.[28] As a result, there was not a great incentive to conduct similar activities as the East Donegal Memorialists. It is unknown what the Loyalist community in Cavan and Monaghan thought of the East Donegal Memorial. The local newspapers in these counties, the *Anglo-Celt* and *Northern Standard*, never reported the Memorial despite other local newspapers doing so – including the *Sligo Champion*, *Offaly Independent*, *Wicklow People* and *Cork Examiner*.[29] Perhaps these newspapers did not report the Memorial to prevent local Loyalists committing similar actions, which could have created unrest and wrath from the Free State government. Community relations were a serious concern in these counties, especially as the tradition of the Twelfth (of July) demonstrations in these counties ended in 1931 following the Newtowngore and Cootehill riots.[30]

The Gardaí began to suspect the Memorial originated from the local Unionist Northern Counties Club in Derry/Londonderry, according to a report from 1 December. A deputation met the minister of agriculture of Northern Ireland, Sir Basil Brooke, concerning the grievances of the east Donegal dairy farmers. The deputation consisted of Dr Joseph Alexander, a solicitor in Derry/Londonderry, and a dairy farmer in Carrigans where he resided. The rest were dairy farmers, Thomas Boyd Rankin, Robert W. Glenn, Thomas Orr and J. McElwaine from Carrigans.[31]

The Gardaí suspected members of the CDPRA from 15 November as the instigators, including Myles. They found no definite evidence to connect him to the Memorial, though they noted he spent much of his time in Derry/Londonderry, often going to the Unionist Northern Counties Club and taking part in Remembrance Day commemorations in the city.[32] He was a known ex-Unionist and a member of the CDPRA that represented their interest in the Dáil. Nevertheless, the major's involvement in the Memorial is highly doubtful for two reasons. He never presented evidence to the Boundary Commission or spoke in favour of Donegal Unionists being transferred to Northern Ireland, as he was from Ballyshannon, an area the Boundary Commission never considered to cede to Northern Ireland, due to its geographic position and the population of the local area primarily being Catholic. Furthermore, he was a TD of the county, and would remain so whether or not the Boundary line changed. If he voiced any opinion on the matter he could alienate both his constituency's electorate and elements of the Free State government that could cut him out of certain committees.[33]

The Gardaí also suspected others of being involved in the Memorial, such as Lieutenant-Colonel Hart from Kilderry, since 15 November, and their suspicions could be understood.[34] He held great influence and the respect of many Loyalists in east Donegal, coming from a prominent landowning family that had held their estate since the Plantation of Ulster. He had served in the British Army since 1899, and following the First World War he retired from the military and focused on community affairs. He was appointed as deputy lieutenant in Co. Donegal in 1921, became a member of the CDPRA that presented evidence to the Boundary Commission in 1925, and remained a prominent landowner in the region. Hart had influence within the Church of Ireland as well by being a member of the Derry and Raphoe diocesan synod, a member the general synod, and a prominent member of the select vestry of the Muff parish church.[35] Thus he had the necessary influence that the Memorialists desired to convince east Donegal Protestants to back the petition, but what would be his motivation? Large estate owners, who were predominantly Protestant, still held large stretches of land in the county. Okan Ozseker points out that by 1923 Sir John Leslie possessed 12,000 acres of untenanted land, while the earl of Leitrim held 39,000 acres. By 1925, two years following the Land Act 1923, the earl of Leitrim's estate was reduced by more than half, due to the Land Commission buying out the land. By the Land Act 1933, some Protestant landowners felt they could not tolerate any further land acts. The British government had introduced land acts from 1870 to 1919; thus the Free State government was not conducting affairs drastically differently, yet this latest act was one of the factors that led to the start of the Economic War. It diverted land annuities that originally went to the British government for repayment of earlier land acts that broke up much of the large landowner estates in Ireland since 1870, to be utilized for local government projects instead.

During this period big Irish houses had struggled to survive and felt they had reached their limit by both the new act and the Anglo-Irish trade war.[36] The matter of land annuities was a national issue, affecting smallholding Protestant and Catholic farmers alike with financial burden, especially along the border, and the Free State economy heavily depended on agriculture. Peadar O'Donnell had been campaigning to end the land annuities since 1925, and was still doing so when the East Donegal Memorial was being reported.[37] Hart had lost much through partition. Katherine Magee notes that in the mid-nineteenth century the Hart family owned 6,598 acres in Co. Donegal, while across in Co. Londonderry they had only 434 acres. Most of the land in Donegal was broken up and sold by the Land Commission. Despite this, a bigger pain to his family was their ancestral home, Kilderry House, in Co. Donegal near Muff. The family had to relocate to Ballynagard House in 1928 for political reasons; the property was just seven miles away across the border in Co. Londonderry. It was not just a matter of the amount of land their estate lost, but the quality of their home as well. As Magee notes, Hart had written letters to his wife complaining about the quality of the land at Ballynagard. In addition, the family had a timber business in Kilderry, selling Scotch Firs to the Harland and Wolff shipyard in Belfast, with border customs now hampering his business.[38] If the Memorial successfully altered the border then Kilderry House, its surrounding farming estate and his timber business would be ceded to Northern Ireland. If Hart was indeed in league with the Memorialists, he would be fundamental to gathering much-needed support for their cause in the Muff area. There is evidence of this, as canvassing for the Memorial was first reported in the area with Acheson potentially involved on his behalf. The border village of Muff and its surrounding area, which had a Protestant majority, was to be transferred under the recommendation of the Boundary Commission.[39]

By 1 December the Gardaí's list of suspected members increased further to include dairy farmers John Neely from Newtown-cunningham, T. Wylie from Moville and Andre Lowrey from Lifford, as well as solicitors from Raphoe called McNulty and Wilson. It also included high-profile figures such as Major Moore, Edward Sullivan Murphy, MP for the city of Londonderry, and Gilbert Magee who was son of the former mayor of the Londonderry Borough Corporation, John Gilbert Magee. In addition, Samuel Alexander Baxter and Wagentreiber were on the list, independent Protestant councillors who were on the Donegal County Council. Another independent Protestant councillor on the Donegal County Council and campaign agent for Myles, Scott, was also suspected from 15 November.[40] Scott was the honorary secretary for the CDPRA. He submitted testimonies and evidence by Donegal Unionists to the

Boundary Commission to support their claims to include areas of east and south Donegal into Northern Ireland, which influenced the Boundary Commission Report in 1925.[41]

This suspicion of the independent Protestant councillors was brought up in the Donegal County Council on 27 November 1934. At the meeting, Scott raised an issue concerning the council-operated minor-relief schemes, noting an unfair allocation of grants in the county.[42] Out of £12,610 that had been granted under the scheme in 1934, Dunfanaghy got £2,345 and Glenties got £4,480, 54.1 per cent of the entire grant. In comparison, in east Donegal £60 was allocated for a bog road in the area of the former rural district of Londonderry no. 2, and the former rural district of Strabane no. 2 received nothing. In the year prior, Dunfanaghy and Glenties got £8,755 out of £13,877 (63.1 per cent) of similar grants, while the Londonderry no. 2 and Strabane no. 2 areas got nothing, and this was a pattern that had been going on for many years. Scott described the situation: 'It is difficult for even the meekest Moses, which I don't profess to be, to refrain from strong language of the superlative adjectival type in considering this allocation, but I will confine myself to saying it is most unfair'.[43] He put forward the motion:

> The Commissioners of Public Works be requested to give some consideration in future allocation of relief grants to Aileach (Londonderry no. 2) and the former Strabane no. 2 areas, and that the attention of the commissioners be directed to their letter of August last wherein it was stated that due consideration would be given to claims of these areas.[44]

Councillor Baxter, though an independent Protestant councillor, did remind those present that in earlier years of the council up to £60,000 was spent in Londonderry no. 2 and Strabane no. 2, while Milford got barely any funding. Therefore, the current status quo was just making matters equal, but Scott pointed out that 'anything we got under other grants we paid for'. Despite these comments, the motion was passed and the debate revealed a high level of discontentment in areas in east Donegal with the Donegal County Council in regard to the allocation of public funding.[45]

Later in the meeting a letter was read from Moore, complaining of damage on his property by cattle being smuggled across the border at night. He wished to know what the council would provide him with in terms of compensation and protection from future illegal activity on his lands. After the letter was read, the chairman responded that the matter was for the Gardaí, not the county council. Scott suggested the council should write to the major informing him the issue was not within their jurisdiction. He knew of Moore's property in Ballyshannon, Cliff Lodge, and recalled when Moore tried to include the property in Northern Ireland during the time of the Boundary Commission. It was at this point of the meeting that Fianna Fáil councillor, Patrick Lynch, challenged Scott's involvement in the Memorial in the light of his involvement in the Boundary Commission and of his complaints of the situation in east Donegal. Lynch said to Scott 'I suppose you signed your name to the recent document', to which Scott responded 'For once in your life you are wrong, Mr Lynch'. None of the other independent Protestant councillors present at the meeting were questioned on their involvement with the Memorial, and no other councillor asked any further questions or made statements. The matter was dropped and this remained the only time the Memorial was discussed at the Donegal County Council.[46]

Nonetheless, these suspicions were partly correct: elements of the CDPRA and Orange Order *had* been making plans since at least July 1934. They had the network and support base to quickly galvanize the former Unionist community to sign such a petition, with experienced members to organize and collect signatures from the time of the Ulster Covenant. As journalists travelled to east Donegal to report the event and interview local Protestants, they were met with complete silence, demonstrating that the pledge of secrecy had been enforced to the strictest degree. A *Derry Journal* reporter was able to ascertain that the organizers of the Memorial were 'influential agents of the Unionist party', likely referring to members of the CDPRA.[47] This is known from the letters sent to the Irish Loyalist Imperial Federation in London.

The Federation was formed in November 1933, and had evolved from the London branch of the Irish Unionist Alliance that remained active during the 1920s despite the dissolution of the party. The organization's purpose was to safeguard the constitutional liberties and rights of southern Irish Loyalists.[48] The Federation had connections with the British political establishment, with Sir Edward Carson as its president.[49] The Federation also had an international network with members in the British Isles, Australia, Canada, France, the United States of America, Belgium, India, South Africa and other British colonies. The organization actively challenged de Valera's policies and aspirations for Ireland. In May 1934, a unitary call to all southern Irish-born Loyalists was sent out to defend their constitutional status against these changes, with the Federation 'to take steps as may be necessary for the purpose as occasion arises'. This call may have been one of the catalysts for the organization of a major political demonstration in east Donegal to defend their constitutional rights through a public petition, as they did with the Ulster Covenant in 1912. The Federation was still a small entity, as by 14 August 1934 the organization had 600 to 700 subscribers with £400 in its budget. Nevertheless, the Memorialists must have felt this was the best southern Irish Loyalist-dedicated relief organization in the empire they could turn to for aid. In a letter sent to the Federation on 4 July by the Memorialists' secretary was an attached official copy of a draft Memorial (appendix 1).[50]

The draft memorial had inconsistencies, as some figures were exaggerated to help the Memorialists' case, such as their claim Donegal Loyalists paid 85 per cent of the entire rates in the county by 1934. When they claimed they 'own 90 per cent of the property in this area and we consolidate at 75 per cent of the population', they do not state which area they mean. Under the 1911 census, just 38 per cent of residents in the former Westminster constituency of East Donegal were Protestant.[51] In both the rural district councils of Londonderry no. 2 and Strabane no. 2, Protestants made up respectively 49 and 48 per cent of the population. In the Laggan Valley, the heartland of east Donegal Protestants, Catholics made up 53 per cent of the population and this had increased by 1934.[52] Another example of these figures being exaggerated is the claim that 35,000 Donegal Loyalists were signatories of the Ulster Covenant and Declaration; this figure was closer to 18,000. Even if this was the case, and every Protestant in the county had signed the Covenant as they believed, their Memorial focused on east Donegal. For the Westminster constituency of East Donegal, only a total of 8,553 signatories were obtained.[53]

4. Thomas Boyd Rankin (photograph generously provided by John Rankin)

The document, though in its infancy as a draft, laid out their name from the start, the Memorialists. The organizers estimated the document would represent 5,000 Loyalists, and the most important element of all is that at the bottom of the document there were six signatures, granting insight into who were the original instigators.[54] The first was Thomas Boyd Rankin, a farmer from Cloon (fig. 4). Prior to the Home Rule crisis, he was a leader within the St Johnston LOL no. 992 and was the worshipful master of the St Johnston Royal Black Preceptory no. 134.[55] He was a UVF company commander and a standing committee member of the Co. Donegal Unionist Association, a position he likely maintained when the organization evolved into the CDPRA.[56] He was elected onto Londonderry no. 2 as a Unionist from 1911 to 1920, when he decided to not stand for re-election.[57] In the 1925 local election, he and John Black were nominated to stand for the county council in the local electoral area

5. William Robert Glenn (photograph generously provided by Marion Bennett)

of Buncrana as independent Protestant candidates. Boyd did not gain a seat; however, his colleague did, ensuring Protestant representation from Buncrana on the county council.[58] By 5 December the Gardaí suspected Dr Alexander of being the instigator of the Memorialists, and this was incorrect. He was on every deputation to the Northern government, with Rankin there alongside him every time. Alexander may have been the east Donegal farmer's solicitor, but Rankin was certainly a key figure in these deputation talks, meaning he had a level of authority among the Memorialists.[59] As a dairy farmer, and not an elected politician, he was not suspected by the Gardaí.

The second signatory was John Sheppard Weir, a farmer from Lifford with a family-run auctioneering firm in Strabane, Alex Weir & Co. Prior to partition, he was the secretary and treasurer of the Strabane Farmers' Union, and justice of the peace for both Donegal and Tyrone.[60] After partition, he lost his influence in local

6. James Taylor Fleming (photograph generously provided by George Fleming)

government, and the border caused him many business issues through customs checks. Third was Robert William Glenn, a farmer and milk vendor from Carrigans (fig. 5).[61] He was involved in the county's National Farmers' and Ratepayers' League, a member of the Finance Committee of the North West Agricultural Society, and vice-chairman of the Killia-Carrigans branch of the Donegal Unionist Association in 1920 that later became the CDPRA.[62] These positions meant he knew in great detail how dire the Economic War had made the east Donegal farmers, and he held a level influence and respect among them. Glenn was also the treasurer of the Presbyterian Monreagh Church and a member of the Session; it is possible he used his connections within the Presbyterian Church to get members of the clergy to support the Memorial and encourage their congregations to do the same.[63]

7. William John Greer Throne (photograph generously provided by Mary Hamilton)

The fourth signature was James Taylor Fleming, an engineer from St Johnston and an active figure in community affairs, being deeply involved in the Masonic and Orange orders (fig. 6).[64] He supported the Memorial for similar reasons as the fifth signatory, William John Greer Throne, a farmer from Portinure and worshipful master of the Lifford LOL no. 1860 since 1922 (fig. 7).[65] During the Irish Civil War, Anti-Treaty Irish Republican Army forces commandeered the Lifford Orange Hall from June to July 1922, causing malicious damage to the property.[66] These events convinced many of their members to migrate to Northern Ireland; their membership continued to fall, as young people chose to look for work across the border, possibly due to the requirement of understanding and speaking Irish for some jobs in the county, such as teaching or the civil service.[67] The Lifford Orange Hall continued to suffer from harassment over the years; in 1929, the walls of the Hall were painted green and inscriptions such as 'Up Dublin' were written all over. When the case was brought to court a year later, the incident caused amusement and laughter, primarily from the district justice. He did not take the case seriously, making jokes such as 'Green paint on an Orange Hall! That is the unkindest cut of all'. He dismissed the case, ruling that there was no evidence to make the charge.[68] Considering that Lifford is just across the border, it is understandable that Throne would back the Memorial as a means to safeguard his local Protestant community from authorities he did not trust. Throne and Fleming served as district master and deputy district master of Raphoe District LOL no. 3, and held the same roles in the Raphoe Black Chapter District no. 3.[69] At this time, Raphoe District LOL no. 3 of the City of Derry Grand Orange Lodge had lodges in Carrigans, Convoy, Lifford, Manorcunningham, Newtowncunningham, Raphoe, St Johnston and Stranorlar. East Donegal had Orange lodges in Burt and Castlefin as well, which belonged to the jurisdictions of the City of Derry District LOL no. 1 and the County Tyrone Grand Orange Lodge as part of Castlederg District LOL respectively.[70] By 1936 these east Donegal lodges had approximately 550 members in total.[71] Throne and Fleming would have been able to contact these lodges, providing the Memorialists a vital network across most of east Donegal to gather signatures and gain volunteers to their cause. No minute books remain for the Raphoe District LOL no. 3 during this era; there is circumstantial evidence that the local Orange Order was involved due to dates for district meetings. Unlike lodge meetings that take place each month, district meetings take place four times a year. This is usually in January, April, June and October, which coincided with key events for the Memorialists. A letter was sent to the Irish Loyalist Imperial Federation on 4 July, with a draft copy of the Memorial. A few weeks earlier a district meeting was held in June, and the Memorialists could have discussed their idea of a border petition, to see if the worshipful masters of the other lodges supported their proposal. Canvassing for signatures began in early November, and prior to this another district meeting was held in October, in which the Memorialists could have organized this canvasing of signatures with the local leaders of the order. Although the evidence is circumstantial, the dates do fit a general pattern.

8. Matthew Kerr (*Derry Standard*, 7 Nov. 1934)

The final signatory was Samuel McClintock, an extensive farmer from Lurgybrack, Letterkenny. He was a member of an old and highly respected family in the county, and ran the family's foundry business in Letterkenny.[72] All the instigators were Presbyterians, had signed the Ulster Covenant, and felt the Memorial was the best course to improve their situations.

Fleming, acting as the Memorialists' secretary, was the one who sent the official copy of the draft Memorial to the Federation. He also sent a copy to the parliamentary secretary at the Ministry of Home Affairs in Northern Ireland, George Hanna, on 27 July 1934. They asked for advice on its presentation, assurances of interest and support on the matter. Even at this stage, Fleming asked that any correspondence on the subject be addressed to him, c/o Matthew Kerr in Derry/Londonderry (fig. 8).[73] Kerr was a valuable ally, for he was the grandmaster of the City of Derry Grand Orange Lodge, governor of the Apprentice Boys, a justice of the peace, and a Unionist councillor on the Londonderry Borough Corporation.[74] Correspondence went through Kerr to prevent letters being intercepted by Republicans working in the Free State Post Office.

Fleming had been in communication with the Federation since June, in particular with John E. Walsh and the Federation's acting secretary. These letters do show some issues that arose during this period of correspondence going through Kerr, as there was a delay in responding to letters in some cases or letters not being received at all. For example, in late June to early July, Fleming wrote to the Federation concerning their Memorial with an attached draft copy and asked to address any correspondence c/o Matthew Kerr. The Federation responded by early July, enquiring whether their petition had yet been presented and, if so, on what date, and what was the response to its presentation. It appears Fleming did not get the letter as he then sent nearly the exact same letter and draft Memorial that he had sent George Hanna on 27 July, asking for help and support and again to address any correspondence c/o Matthew Kerr. The only difference was he added a postscript at the bottom of the letter enquiring how to both join the Federation and create a local branch within east Donegal. Then later in a letter from Fleming to John E. Walsh, sent on 3 August, he apologized for not responding sooner due to a family bereavement and being unable to travel to Derry/ Londonderry until the day he sent a reply. Fleming then told Walsh he had received a letter from the Federation's acting secretary and that a representative would be in the city during the first fortnight of that month, which Fleming hoped was him, as he wanted the opportunity of interesting Walsh in 'the cause of the Loyalists of this district'.[75]

During this time, internal letters within the Federation dating 1, 9 and 14 August show confusion with Fleming, as they began to have questions with their correspondence with Fleming. Why did he not respond to their letter from early July? Why were some of the letters typewritten, in pencil, or looked like they came off a duplicator? Why did he send two copies of the draft memorial in two letters? Why did he need assurances of their support, and for what? They assumed this section was not originally meant for them but a copy that was sent to someone else, as they did not understand why Fleming requested their assistance and advice on the Memorial's presentation. Members of the Federation began to question if their letters to Fleming were being interfered with, whether by Matthew Kerr, the addressee or someone else. They wanted to clarify that Fleming was getting their letters before they proceeded any further or provided any detailed information. This concern of their being intercepted can be seen within letters between Federation members, as no full names or locations are given. As John E. Walsh is written as 'Mr W.', while Fleming is known as 'Mr F.', 'Mr. J.T.F.' or 'our friend in D'. So even the Federation treated knowledge of the Memorial with secrecy at its earliest stages, in the same fears as the Memorialists to prevent intelligence being leaked to Irish Republican circles and protect the identities of those involved.[76]

After Fleming responded to the Federation's secretary on 3 August, he gave his organization some answers, and he received a response on 14 August. He conveyed his sympathy for Fleming's family loss, and told Fleming he was unsure if he had received all the letters that were sent via Kerr. They informed him of their first response letter from early July not being responded to, and that the secretary intentionally did not respond to Fleming's letter on 27 July. Unsure if Fleming had sent this, or someone had sent this on his behalf, he asked why Fleming wanted to be assured of their sympathy and support before presenting the Memorial. The letter then gave Fleming and the Memorialists encouraging news. The Federation's acting secretary wrote that the Federation's Executive Committee would be obliged if Fleming let them know if there would be any objection of the Memorial receiving any publicity, without the Memorialists' names or addresses being given. In addition, the Federation secretary sent another letter to Fleming with forms for him to join the Federation, with some information pamphlets on the Federation. This showed that the Federation were happy to help, and use the Donegal Loyalists' petition as a publicity opportunity against the Free State government.[77] In Northern Ireland, in comparison, after a series of correspondence, by 5 September the letter was brought forward to the minister of home affairs and the prime minister of Northern Ireland who recommended Hanna to take no action.[78]

According to the *Irish Times*, the petition was drawn up in Strabane.[79] This would have made sense; the town is on the border, a location easy for the East Donegal Memorialists to reach and feel secure. If this was the case, the timing of Fleming's first letter to the Irish Imperialist Federation in June suggests the draft Memorial may have been written sometime near when the Grand Orange Lodge of Ireland held their general half-yearly meeting on 13 June. This was the first time such a meeting took place in Strabane and witnessed a large attendance, including representatives from across the Free State. Neither Throne nor Fleming was present, yet Matthew Kerr was. Revd Moriarty was present at the meeting as well, and his attendance may have influenced his speech to the Free State Orangemen the following month.[80] This is because following the meeting an afternoon luncheon took place at the Strabane YMCA, hosted by the County Tyrone Grand Orange Lodge, and a number of speeches were made. The most prominent was by James F. Gamble, MP for the Northern Ireland parliament constituency of North Tyrone. He declared they (the Orange brethren) came to Strabane, to his constituency, and were very near to a very loyal part of Donegal. Down along the banks of the Foyle they had many loyal brethren who were proud to be associated with the order and who had never sullied the colours they wore. He hoped the time would come when they would be able to meet their brethren in the Free State with the border swept away, not with them swept into the Free State, but with the new parliament buildings housing representatives from the south who would be proud to belong to the British Empire.[81] Gamble was openly suggesting an alteration of the boundary, being met with a round of applause by those present, yet he does not explain how this was to come about. For Gamble this was important, as he said Tyrone was a large county, but unfortunately had only two representatives in the Northern Irish parliament that 'dig with the right foot'. The *Derry Journal* was greatly suspicious of his words and wrote an article believing an endeavour of some kind was being quietly pursued to bring in these Donegal Orangemen as they 'dig with the right foot', but had no evidence of what this was.[82] It is unknown if Gamble or Revd Moriarty knew of the Memorialists' plans. An east Donegal border petition was never discussed at the meeting, according to the annual report, yet it could have been discussed off the record or at a different gathering that might have occurred near the time, when many prominent Ulster Unionist and Orange leaders were in Strabane.

By 14 November a Memorial was delivered originally to the Irish Loyalist Imperial Federation. They then passed this to the British and Northern Irish governments, and the news was announced to the press.[83] The Memorialists had forwarded their petition, in regards to the final text, to the federation nearly a month prior. The timing of the Memorial was important as it marked an important meeting of the Federation on 14 November. The meeting marked the first anniversary of its founding at a well-attended event at Caxton Hall in London. At the meeting, the Federation passed a resolution calling on the British government to declare their intentions towards de Valera's government, which had repeatedly violated the Anglo-Irish Treaty. In their view, the actions of Westminster towards these violations were either cowardly appeasement or callous indifference, with safeguards for southern Unionists being systematically abolished.[84] The timing also served the Memorialists' interests, as the meeting drew more attention to the concerns of the southern Irish Loyalists

9. Officers of the City of Derry Grand Orange Lodge, 5 Nov. 1934
(*Derry Standard*, 7 Nov. 1934)

and it was near Armistice Day, a reminder of the wartime sacrifice
of Donegal Unionists. Another important event occurred for east
Donegal and Derry/Londonderry city Orangemen as well. Just
over a week previously, on 5 November, it was the centenary of
the establishment of the City of Derry Grand Orange Lodge and
a celebration was held in the Guildhall of the city.[85] This was an
important event for the Memorialists, as many important local figures
were there that the Memorialists could make contact with to gain
support for their movement. This can be seen in the photograph of
William Throne and James T. Fleming with Matthew Kerr, Edward
S. Murphy and Sir Dudley Evelyn Bruce McCorkell, the lord mayor
of the City of Derry/Londonderry (fig. 9).[86] How many of the
officers in this photograph knew of the Memorialists' plans prior to
it becoming public knowledge for the press, or took an active role?
The Federation meeting, Armistice Day, and the City of Derry
Grand Orange Lodge Centenary raised the profile of the Unionists
of east Donegal; during this period the Memorialists would have had
the most sympathy and support for their movement, especially when
gathering signatures for their petition. This can be seen with the date
of centenary celebrations, which coincides with witness reports of
the first day canvassing took place for signatures of the Memorial.

Signings of the Memorial appeared to be a bigger success than originally anticipated when creating the draft, with 7,368 signatories (appendix 2).[87] The Memorial deeply expressed their emotions, feeling besieged and unfairly treated by people wishing to 'filch' their lands. The wording is nearly the same as the draft Memorial that was created in June, but with subtle differences. There is more emphasis on east Donegal Protestantism than on Loyalists, to make it more specific who they are. This creates an appearance that they are suffering from religious and cultural discrimination, as well as political. They use the word 'pray' more, giving the impression they are desperately on their hands and knees pleading. There is a much greater reference to the king or the monarch in this version than in the draft – 'loyal subjects of the king as in former and happier times' – in hopes of remedying their affairs. But the biggest difference is that there are no claims of threats of violence against them, or how they felt the Gardaí were unable or unwilling to help them. It is unknown why this was not included; perhaps they did not wish to anger the local Gardaí if their efforts were in vain, or such harassment was hard to prove and so they focused purely on the issues that they had evidence to grieve about.[88] Nevertheless, copies of the draft Memorial were obtained by the British and Irish press and published from 14 to 15 November in the *Derry Journal*, the *Derry Standard*, the *Irish Times*, the *Belfast News-Letter* and the *Londonderry Sentinel*.[89] This made the East Donegal Memorial known across Ireland and Great Britain. There were reports the Memorial was sent to the League of Nations as well.[90] Archives of the League show no petition concerning Donegal had ever been sent, but many in Ireland and Great Britain did not know this and still thought the matter had been raised at the highest body in the international community. This put more pressure on British and Irish politicians to take the matter seriously.

2. Reactions within the British Empire

News of the East Donegal Memorial quickly spread to numerous local and national newspapers across Ireland, Great Britain and the British Empire. Articles on the Memorial appeared in newspapers in Australia, New Zealand, South Africa and Southern Rhodesia through correspondents in London and Dublin.[1] Many South African and Southern Rhodesian newspapers that reported the Memorial were known to circulate in neighbouring British protectorates and colonies at this time. This includes Bechuanaland, Basutoland, Swaziland, Northern Rhodesia and South-African-administered South West Africa.[2] The Memorial was not reported in any newspapers in North America, despite the large Irish diaspora. The *Sentinel and Orange and Protestant Advocate*, the Grand Orange Lodge of British America newspaper (the combined Canadian and Newfoundland Orange Order), may have reported the Memorial, but there are no remaining archives from 1934–5 to verify this.[3] The Irish Loyalist Imperial Federation's half-yearly newsletter, *Notes From Ireland*, reported the Memorial in May 1935.[4] This was because its November 1934 edition was published prior to the events of the East Donegal Memorial;[5] however, news of the Memorial would have reached its international members that subscribed to the newsletter, along with international subscribers of British and Irish newspapers, further spreading knowledge of the Memorialists.

It is surprising no American, Canadian or Newfoundlander newspapers reported the Memorial, for two reasons. First, due to the large Irish diaspora in these nations, many newspapers often wrote about Irish affairs. For instance, the *New York Times* reported when Donegal considered contesting a Unionist candidate during the Southern Ireland general election in 1921, yet it did not report a 7,368-strong petition to alter the Irish border.[6] The articles that were reported in the newspaper from November to December 1934 concerning Ireland included the governor of Northern Ireland being reappointed, the Irish Citizenship Bill, de Valera's response to comments made by the secretary of state for Dominion Affairs, and Northern Ireland being in favour of the Free State being declared a republic.[7] The *New York Times* did report the Irish Loyalist Imperial Federation meeting in London, but briefly.[8] The second reason is that some Canadian and Newfoundland newspapers supported the imperial connection of their dominions with the UK and the British Empire. The Toronto-based *Evening Telegram* had a weekly page in its Saturday edition concerning British news, 'Echoes from the Motherland'.[9] Among the reasons the East Donegal Memorial was not reported in North America may have been, first, the strong pro-Irish Republican attitudes of the American and some Canadian newspapers at this time.[10] Another factor was that Canada had begun the process of distancing its connections with the UK through the Statute of Westminster in 1931, making Canada a sovereign state in its own right, and the reporting style of Canadian newspapers had begun to reflect this by becoming more indifferent to British news.[11] It is in part due to this that the Canadian Press, a news agency founded in 1917 as a distribution network of information across the country, may have heard of the Memorial but did not distribute it widely.[12] In addition, the struggle for Irish Home Rule then independence caused community issues in Canada and Newfoundland. There were clashes between Irish communities who supported Ulster Unionists or Irish Nationalists, particularly during partition.[13] It is possible that the Canadian press agency did not distribute news of the Memorial for fear that any question of the future of the Irish boundary could have potentially stirred up troubles that had been put to rest a decade prior.

Most of the press reported the Memorial obtained 8,000 signatures, but other figures were published. The way the press reported the Memorial often reflected the newspaper's political leanings. The Nationalist *Derry Journal*, for example, said that the Memorial originally claimed to represent 5,000 Loyalists, based on the original draft Memorial, while the more Unionist *Irish Times* asserted 8,500 and the Irish edition of the *Daily Express* claimed 10,000.[14] The *Derry Journal* wrote an article concerning this fact among the reporting of the Memorial by the press, to cast doubt on its true signature strength.[15] Even the Memorial's claimed 7,368 signatories could be disputed as no evidence remains of the complete list of signatures, so it is impossible to confirm the true count. After interviewing local Donegal farmers, McManus claimed the number was exaggerated and was a propaganda stunt to gain special treatment by the Northern Irish government for east Donegal dairy farmers. Moreover, it was a counter-blast of Ulster Unionists' published intention of governing and legislating 'as a Protestant government for a Protestant people'. The only confirmation that the Memorial took place is witness accounts of canvassers by journalists and the Gardaí.[16]

Both the *Derry Weekly News* and the *Donegal Vindicator* called the crisis the 'Partition of Donegal scare' and refused to write any articles on the Memorial, stating they would have a 'wait-and-see' policy as they had no faith the Memorialists would be successful.[17] Other Co. Donegal newspapers held similar thoughts. The *Donegal Democrat* published the headline 'UNIONIST PLOT TO PARTITION DONEGAL', while the *Derry People & Tirconaill News* had the headline 'LATEST UNIONIST STUNT', suggesting it was not a serious affair.[18] The *Londonderry Sentinel* and the *Derry Journal* used the topic to fuel their ongoing rivalry. When the *Journal* reported the Memorial on 12 November in a double-column article, the *Sentinel* initially believed the story was a hoax.[19] The editor decided to reprint the article the following day with the headline 'DONEGAL LOYALISTS – *DERRY JOURNAL* DISCOVERS A PLOT' to make political humour of the newspaper's journalism and cast doubt on the Memorial's actual existence.[20] The *Journal* responded to this mockery through a two-step approach. The following day, the *Journal* published the full text of the draft Memorial before the *Sentinel* published it, despite the secrecy observed among Donegal's Protestant community.[21] According to Garda reports, however, the *Journal* never acquired a copy of the Memorial. Instead, a reporter from the *Sentinel* got it from a Donegal farmer visiting Derry/Londonderry, and allowed a *Journal* reporter to make shorthand notes of its contents, for a consideration.[22] Then, on 16 November, the *Journal* criticized the *Sentinel* in an article headlined 'PREMATURELY UNMASKED' for believing the story was fake, and used the *Sentinel*'s own words against it from the previous articles. As on 13 November, the *Sentinel* agreed with the *Journal* in calling the character of Donegal Unionists 'deeply sinister', claiming de Valera's government would have a right to find the 'thieving plotters' who attempted to 'steal' any territory and deal with them according to the law.[23] Perhaps the *Sentinel* wrote this as, even though they believed it was a hoax, they wanted to subliminally scare Northern Irish Nationalists from trying to undertake similar actions. This was a clear show of irony that a Unionist newspaper criticized other Unionists and sided with de Valera's government against them, a contradictory notion and an embarrassment for the *Sentinel*.

10. District Justice Louis Joseph Walsh (*Irish Independent*, 16 Nov. 1934)

As time passed, the Memorialists felt the issue was not raising sufficient attention. On the night of 27 November, Alexander, John Neely and Thomas Boyd Rankin met Edward S. Murphy at the Northern Counties Club in Derry/ Londonderry. It was at this meeting that the Gardaí suspected a new Memorial was drafted, without anyone signing this document.[24] Two days later, on 29 November, a second Memorial, acting as an addendum to the first, was sent and presented by the Irish Loyalist Imperial Federation to the British and Northern Irish governments, and the secretary of state for Dominion Affairs, James Henry Thomas (appendix 3).[25]

The second Memorial included new details of their plight, and suggestions on how to alleviate their situation. They requested, if their region was not transferred to Northern Ireland, for a commission of inquiry into their situation and to exchange their farmlands with Northern Irish Nationalists or for land in England. They pointed out the British government's intervention in international affairs, including altering borders. Making their pleas appear more practical strengthened their case. They compared themselves to Jews travelling to Palestine – a religious minority seeking to return to an ancient homeland deeply rooted into their community, as Ulster was to them. They again made themselves appear desperate, pleading 'grant the prayer of this memorial'. These new requests were made as a response to threats. They received a warning from the District Justice Louis Joseph Walsh from his court at Letterkenny (fig. 10).[26] He claimed the Memorialists were guilty of treasonable practices, and released a statement to the press on 15 November from Letterkenny Court (appendix 4).[27]

Walsh had a history of bias towards the Irish state in legal matters. When the issue of fishing rights in Lough Foyle was first raised, in October 1923, he declared the waters belonged to the Free State while ministers on both sides of the border were unsure of the constitutional position.[28] On another occasion, a few months prior to the Memorial being announced, he spoke in Belfast of what wonderful people Ulster Protestants could be if they converted to 'the Faith'.[29] Walsh was a constitutional Nationalist until the 1916 Easter Rising, and then stood as a Sinn Féin candidate for South Londonderry in the 1918 general election.[30] During the Irish War of Independence, British soldiers raided his office and put him on the run until he was caught, whereupon he went through internment in both Derry/Londonderry jail and Ballykinlar camp in 1921.[31] When he heard of the Memorial, Walsh believed there would be severe consequences for the Memorialists and threatened war in Ireland. In his view, the only way they could achieve their Unionist desires would be through the British government, and any attempt to seize territory would risk a new war in Europe for 'a few anti-Irish bigots in St Johnston and Burt'.[32]

The Memorialists made the addendum as a response to Walsh's comments, to allow an alternative option to be present. An interesting note concerning this second Memorial is that only Robert W. Glenn and Thomas Boyd Rankin signed the document;[33] this suggests that some of the original draft Memorial signatories either found it difficult to congregate to sign the new memorial or decided to no longer be part of the movement. This may have been due to concerns for their safety, as they did not like the attention that the campaign was getting, especially the open threats that the judge had made. By 5 December local reporters in the area found it harder to gain information in east Donegal, reflecting how concerned residents were of making any comments on the Memorial. A reporter of the *Irish Times* felt 'the Laggan has become a valley of whispers'. There were rumours that the Free State government planned to take proceedings against the organizers of the Memorials, and there was concern that open discussions by anyone involved with the movement would harm their relations with their Catholic neighbours.[34]

The Memorialists who did persevere with the movement made attempts to raise awareness of their campaign, with several newspapers across the UK and Ireland publicizing their plight. These included several letters to the editors of Unionist newspapers from ordinary Northern Irish residents that sympathized with the Memorialists.[35] There were some letters that were written by Donegal Protestants highlighting their plight, supporting the Memorial's case, or condemning Walsh. But they never gave their names to protect themselves; they signed their letters as 'LAGANEER', 'INISHOWEN' or 'A COUNTY DONEGAL PROTESTANT' instead.[36] In several events held by Ulster Unionists, local politicians raised the issue of east Donegal to their counterparts. Captain William Henderson Fyffe, joint secretary of the Tyrone and Fermanagh Unionist Association, held a talk on 23 November at the Clogher branch of the South Tyrone Women's Unionist Association.[37] The captain was not from Donegal, hailing from Tyrone; he represented the Unionist deputation of counties Tyrone and Fermanagh and gave evidence to the Boundary Commission in 1925 of their desire to be part of Northern Ireland. However, he and the deputation had let the Commission know of their desire for northern Monaghan and east Donegal to come under the government of Northern Ireland. He believed that the men of Donegal had the same spirit of loyalty and patriotism as their brethren in Tyrone, and hoped to see them under the Union flag again.[38]

At the talk in Clogher, Fyffe reminded the Unionists in the association of the dangerous period when their own counties were at risk of being excluded from Northern Ireland due to their significant majority Catholic populations. These counties were not abandoned then, which would have weakened the integrity and security of Northern Ireland, and similarly the Unionists of east Donegal and their predominantly Protestant territory rightfully belonged in Northern Ireland.[39] Fyffe took the opportunity to reply to comments made by District Justice Walsh. He remarked that there would be outrage by Nationalist politicians and their supportive press if a magistrate or judge in Northern Ireland condemned the political actions and speeches of the Nationalist population residing in Northern Ireland, in a manner like that of Walsh. Fyffe continued by saying Walsh never attempted to refute any allegations made against him of unfair treatment, especially the accusation of treason

he made against the Donegal Unionists.[40] He laid the question back to
the district justice: what should happen to the Nationalist politicians
and political activists who for years had been openly campaigning and
planning to make Northern Ireland part of an Irish Republic? Should
they be condemned as traitors too? Fyffe argued that these politicians
had been spared from trials and prosecutions only by the guidance of
the Unionist leaders of Northern Ireland. To Fyffe's mind, however,
this did not happen for his fellow Protestants in the Irish Free State.[41]
He also mentioned the East Donegal Memorial and Walsh at a bazaar
organized by Clabby LOL 387.[42]

Fyffe's example was seen in speeches by other Ulster Unionist
leaders. On 17 November a new Orange hall opened for Fenton's
Invisible LOL no. 1104 near Randalstown, Co. Antrim.[43] Sir Joseph
McConnell, 2nd baronet, Westminster UUP MP for Antrim, used
the occasion to both congratulate the brethren of the lodge for their
new hall and discuss Walsh's statement:

> I noticed the other day that Mr Walsh, whose ordinary duties
> are to administer justice, has certainly been making speeches
> that make one think he is more like 'Handy Andy' than an
> administrator of justice. Mr Walsh's antics in assuming the role
> of 'Handy Andy' to De Valera has made it as embarrassing to his
> chief as Samuel Lover 'Handy Andy' did for this.[44]

He goes on to describe Walsh's speech as 'vapourings', a futile
attempt to both lampoon and deprecate Ulster Unionism. These
jests by the judge reminded him of the sinister intent of a jester at
the court of Ferdinand and Isabella of Spain.[45] If this was the kind of
individual that would usually administer justice in the courts south of
the border, he believed it was another reason for Northern Ireland to
be separate from the Irish Free State.[46]

A few weeks later, on 3 December, an annual meeting was held
of the Carrick Division of the Ulster Women's Unionist Association
at the Ulster Unionist Party Headquarters at Glengall Street, Belfast.
The speakers at the event were both Westminster MPs for Antrim,
McConnell and Sir Hugh O'Neill, and the Stormont MP for Carrick,
John Fawcett Gordon. During the meeting, O'Neill discussed the
changes being undertaken by de Valera's government in the Irish Free

State, especially the Irish Citizenship Bill, which he believed was intended to damage the UK's international reputation. If it were not for the Loyalists in the Irish Free State, whom his heart went out to during this difficult time, he would prefer the Irish government ended 'the nonsense' and finally declare an Irish Republic.[47] McConnell went further, stating their Loyalist friends in Co. Donegal had their sympathy, and if Unionists in Northern Ireland could do anything to help them they would gladly do so. He noticed that this dissatisfaction of where the boundary lay was present among some of Northern Ireland's Nationalists as well, and gave an opportunity for these two groups to swap their farms. He did feel though that he was holding a 'forlorn hope' to their Unionist counterparts in Donegal, as he believed the Nationalists residing in Northern Ireland understood the 'side on which their bread was buttered'.[48]

In the Irish Free State, Walsh was not spared being condemned for his speech concerning the Memorial. On 6 December, in Dáil Éireann, Myles asked the minister for justice, Patrick Joseph Ruttledge, if he was aware of Walsh's recent speech at Letterkenny and what steps the minister proposed to take in response. Major Myles was the independent Protestant TD for Donegal and a member of the CDPRA. Though he may have not been in league with the Memorialists, he still needed to show he would defend his key electoral support base. The minister responded that he was aware of the speech, but did not propose to take any steps. Myles asked the minister if he could tell him whether the speech made by Walsh was meant to incite people in Donegal to commit illegal acts, and whether the minister believed it was correct that an individual in such a position of influence should make a speech from the bench that incited the conduct of unlawful acts. The minister did not want to debate the merits and demerits of the subject. Arguing that the people responsible for organizing the Memorial could be seen as starting incitement, he could not take any disciplinary action against the district justice as the law stood except for dismissing him, a situation he pointed out that Myles already knew. The major continued pressuring the minister, asking if he was correct to assume that the district justice could be called upon to act as a judge in relation to illegal acts that might be committed in Donegal as a by-product of his speech concerning the Memorial and the Unionists of east Donegal. The minister reminded the major he could not take disciplinary action against the district justice besides dismissing him, remarking if this is what the TD desired, then that would be a separate matter. Myles repudiated this remark, stating he was not asking for the individual's dismissal. The minister reminded him of the legal position of the matter, and the last comment made by Myles was that he brought the subject to the minister's attention to stop this kind of behaviour and practice that incites unlawful conduct to the Irish public.[49]

This condemnation of Walsh was not universally shared by all outside of Ireland. The British *Daily Telegraph*, for instance, believed the speech was extraordinary, and its article headline was 'FREE STATE JUSTICE AND A PETITION: AMAZING SPEECH IN COURT'.[50] In the Free State, many saw the judge as a reasonable Irish patriot. The *Irish Independent* had the headline 'THE DONEGAL MEMORIAL: JUSTICE'S STERN WARNING' and the *Connaught Telegraph*: 'DISTRICT JUSTICE'S WARNING: A BORDER PETITION DENOUNCED'.[51] For some newspapers, such as the *Kerry Reporter*, *The Liberator* and the *Donegal Vindicator*, the only time they wrote a news article on the Memorial was when Myles brought forth to the Dáil the matter of the statement made by Walsh. In these articles, and in other Free State and Nationalist newspapers, it turns the narrative of the story from Walsh to Myles. Why was the major bringing the matter to the minister for justice? Was the major not a true Irish patriot?[52] In these articles, they almost give the appearance of a rivalry between the two figures, with the *Connaught Telegraph* having the headline 'T.D. AND JUSTICE', making the reader want to go against the major.[53] This is substantiated in other newspapers, such as the *Evening Herald*, whose sub-headline was 'Minister to "Take no Steps in the Matter"'.[54]

The judge's comments about the Memorial are primarily why the news spread outside the British and Irish Isles. All newspapers that reported the story from the British Empire included Walsh's claims that the document was an act of treason, which could risk a new war in Ireland, that could spread across Europe. This made the story more fascinating for their readers, drawing them in with headlines such as 'TREASON' and 'FREE STATE ARMY MIGHT MARCH'.[55] This is important, as the First World War had ended just sixteen years previously. Millions of troops across the empire were raised to serve overseas during the war and many either were psychologically traumatized, were injured or never came home.[56] Australia, Canada, Newfoundland, New Zealand and South Africa also held large Irish communities. Some of these immigrants experienced the Irish War of Independence and the subsequent Civil War, emigrating as refugees of the conflict or due to economic pressures in the inter-war period.[57] As these conflicts remained in living memory for many across the world, there was understandable apprehension of the idea of any new conflict in Europe. In addition, immigrant Irish Catholics and Protestants held differing stances regarding Ireland and the British Empire, affecting certain political movements within the dominions in which they settled.

News of the Memorial led some international newspapers and groups to sympathize with the Memorialists. The South African *Natal Mercury* ran the headline 'LIVES ENDANGERED UNDER IRISH FREE STATE'.[58] Others began to criticize Walsh, with Ulster Unionists particularly angered by his hypocrisy. Fyffe commented that there would be outrage by Nationalist politicians and their press if a Northern Irish magistrate or judge condemned the political actions of the Nationalist population in a similar manner.[59] The Australian *Daily Telegraph* reported the headline 'WALSH TRAILS HIS COAT'; the Southern Rhodesian *Bulawayo Chronicle* headline was 'ASKING FOR TROUBLE IN IRELAND' and the South African *Cape Argus* headline was 'OUTBURST BY A JUDGE'.[60] Numerous Northern Irish and Commonwealth newspapers often used the phrase 'outburst' in their headlines or articles to describe Walsh's statement, giving the impression he was volatile and irrational when he made his statement. In just a few days following his announcement, the press projected Walsh as an erratic, dishonourable, self-entitled troublemaker and he was condemned at opposite ends of the globe.

There were strong, imperialist factions in these dominions, with many Irish Loyalists continuing to show their British allegiance, as seen with the Irish Loyalist Imperial Federation.[61] The Orange Order had grand lodges in each of these dominions through Irish Protestant immigrants. These were not small branches, as these grand lodges had high memberships. In North America, from 1920 to 1960, 35 per cent of adult Protestant men in Newfoundland were members of the order, and 5–10 per cent of adult Protestant men in Ontario were as well in this period. In relation to Northern Ireland in this same period, this figure was just 20 per cent. These Orange Grand Lodges held great sway with their members holding key political positions in many places. Nearly all the mayors of Toronto up to 1972 were members of the order. In the 1920s, Orangemen made up one-third of the Legislative Assembly of Ontario, and nearly 50 per cent in the General Assembly of Newfoundland. Both Canada and Newfoundland had four prime ministers who were Orangemen, and the New Zealand prime minister from 1912 to 1925, William Massey, was the former grandmaster of the North Island Lodge.[62] During the early twentieth century, their members had pledged loyalty to the king and empire, and to defend the Protestant faith. Thousands of Orangemen served in the First World War to demonstrate their loyalty, as their Irish counterparts did.[63] Despite the distance, they remained strongly connected to Ireland. During the Third Home Rule crisis, the Grand Orange Lodge of Canada had fifty-six members sign the Ulster Covenant, raised over £100,000 in financial aid, and offered volunteers for the UVF in 1914.[64] The East Donegal Memorial had the same effect for some, providing their sympathies to their plight and cause.

Ultimately, Walsh's aggressive stance was counterproductive, adding fuel to the fire for the Memorial by spreading knowledge and sympathy for these Donegal Unionists to the four corners of the globe. If it were not for his statement, it is unlikely the Memorial would have been reported outside the British and Irish Isles. These criticisms did not affect Walsh's judgment, as he remained unapologetic and maintained his stance in a letter to the editor of the *Irish Times* on 21 November, responding to an article they wrote concerning his statement.[65] This was republished in the *Londonderry Sentinel*, *Derry Journal* and *Strabane Weekly News* in the following days (appendix 5).[66]

This would not be the last time District Justice Walsh nearly caused more problems in east Donegal; according to a Garda report on 19 December, Walsh sent a letter to the Free State government suggesting there was a recent concentration of Ulster Special Constabulary units along the Donegal border. He claimed these units were there under the guise of preventing cross-border cattle smuggling, but their true objective was to make an incursion within Co. Donegal to take by force part or the whole of the county. Walsh believed the government needed to respond to this potential threat by establishing a military post of considerable strength. McManus had heard these allegations from Walsh over a week earlier before the report was made. Nevertheless, he made enquiries about any such activity along the border and in Derry/Londonderry. He found no evidence indicative of the activity that Walsh had claimed, and doubted any such activity was likely to happen unless the Northern Irish or British government wished to change the position of the border. McManus reported that Walsh had completely ignored the Gardaí in this matter, and even if such a potential threat were to exist then the whole county would be involved. He believed the establishment of a military post, without a credible threat, would be used by Ulster Unionists for propaganda purposes to increase tension on the position of the Irish border, when the Free State's aim was to reverse this.[67]

3. Responses of the British and Northern Irish governments

Both Memorials were dismissed by the British government, and were not discussed in Westminster. In the parliament of Northern Ireland, the Memorial was discussed on 6 December 1934, when brought forward by Nationalist MP for Foyle, James Joseph McCarroll. He did this in stages, first by making a question to Basil Brooke as the minister of agriculture for Northern Ireland. He asked the minister if he could state the nature of the representations made by the Donegal milk vendors to the ministry in regard to the effects of the Milk and Milk Products Act. What was the response these delegations obtained, and when would the proposed act be put into operation? The minister confirmed he had received representations from Donegal milk vendors, without providing any names or dates, that informed him they would suffer if they were no longer able to sell their milk to Derry/Londonderry. He informed them, after sympathetic and careful consideration, that it would be impractical for the Ministry of Agriculture to authorize the sale of liquid milk on premises outside the jurisdiction of Northern Ireland. Aware that cases of hardship would occur on several farmers in the Irish Free State, he regretted that no other decision was possible and that the act would come into force in a few weeks, on 16 December.[1]

McCarroll then presented a question to the minister of home affairs, Sir Dawson Bates, concerning the Donegal milk vendors. He inquired if the minister was aware of the existence of the East Donegal Memorial and if he could state whether a copy had been received by the government of Northern Ireland. If so, what reply was to be given or action was to be taken by the government and would the document be debated within parliament?[2]

The parliament as a devolved institution did not have the ability to exchange territory, and for Ulster Unionists to open the debate was unthinkable. This could risk encouraging regions with Nationalist majorities in Northern Ireland to demand the same exchange. This was why McCarroll brought the matter forward, and why McCarroll did not discuss the other requests in the Memorial, including a commission or assistance for the transfer of individuals or farmlands.[3] Prior to this debate in Stormont, there had been communication between Nationalist leader Cahir Healy, MP for South Fermanagh in the parliament of Northern Ireland and MP for Fermanagh and Tyrone in Westminster, and Patrick John Little, Fianna Fáil TD for Waterford and parliamentary secretary to De Valera.[4] Little sent Healy a letter a few weeks earlier on 20 November, jolted by the East Donegal Memorialists, who he believed were 'inspired no doubt jointly by the Orange Lodges and by the "Die Hards" of the Carlton Club'. He suggested they obtain signatures for a counter-petition, for the exclusion of all regions within Northern Ireland with a Nationalist majority. He proposed that they make a large display of the movement 'by drum and trumpet', as Unionists had done with the Ulster Covenant in 1912, and threaten to make an appeal to the League of Nations if necessary. Little admitted, in the short term, that initial results could be very slim to nothing. But, in the long term, this could be strategically highly valuable by providing Irish Nationalists an opportunity by creating a 'lever to force open the whole boundary question'.[5] Healy responded on 2 December stating he raised Little's proposal with some of his colleagues. He warned Little it would not be in the interests of the government in Dublin to take much notice of the East Donegal Memorial. If they decided to prosecute anyone it would be counterproductive, stating it is 'just what our masters expect', suggesting it would just serve as Unionist propaganda of the treatment of Protestants in the Free State. Furthermore, he let Little know they were informed that the Saorstát secret service was in the area gathering evidence. Healy admitted they could establish a counter-petition, but only on the condition the Free State government promised to bring it before the League of Nations, and asked if this was possible.[6] Subsequently, this question was never answered; the Northern Irish government was not prepared for the fallout. Minister Bates responded that if McCarroll provided a list of any constituents who wished to emigrate from Northern Ireland, then Stormont would make the arrangements to exchange farms between them and east Donegal Unionists. He appreciated and understood that the number of McCarroll's constituents and Nationalist counterparts who desired to be under Free State jurisdiction would make sufficient room for Donegal and other southern Unionists who wished to once again reside 'under the sheltering folds of the Union Jack'.[7] Edward Murphy inquired of the minister whether he had seen in the newspapers' references to the Memorial that there was a strong desire expressed by these Unionists to be reincorporated into the UK. The minister replied he had and had sympathy for them. John William Nixon, independent Unionist MP for Belfast Woodvale, tried to inquire whether the Stormont government would alter its position back to the Ulster Covenant. Major David Shillington, UUP MP for Central Armagh, interrupted Nixon saying 'no', and the subject was subsequently closed.[8]

The news of the plight of east Donegal Unionists and their Memorials reached the UUC. The council secretary, Sir Wilson Hungerford, MP for Belfast Oldpark, confirmed the council had taken steps to provide assistance to those who wished to take up residence in Northern Ireland via an established fund to give financial aid in buying farmland in the region. The fund was promised several thousand pounds by December 1934.[9] Despite this, some estimated at least £100,000 to £150,000 was needed to achieve success and assistance might have to be in the form of low-interest-rate loans rather than grants, potentially putting these farmers into debt.[10] Another issue with the exchange proposal was that it did not consider non-farmers. For instance, merchants, clerks and solicitors who were as equally Unionist as these Laggan Valley farmers and may have required financial assistance to move to Northern Ireland did not have any farmland to exchange.

The idea of transferring farm holdings was not new. The UUC had set up a central refugee committee on 6 June 1922 to aid southern Unionists who fled to Northern Ireland as a result of the Irish War of Independence and the Civil War that followed, with local refugee committees created in towns.[11] A Loyalist relief fund was established on 19 January 1921, coordinated through a joint committee by the UUC and Ulster Unionist Labour Association; within 48 hours the fund had received 762 applications requesting support.[12] The fund persevered over time until the late 1970s, being used for decades to help southern Irish Protestants migrate to Northern Ireland.[13] There were other similar relief funds and associations, such as the Southern Irish Loyalist Relief Association, the Irish Grants Committee and the Irish Loyalists Association, which functioned for years after partition.[14] By the time of the Memorial, the Church of Ireland and the Presbyterian Church in Northern Ireland were raising funds to establish their own financial schemes to help their co-religionists purchase farms in Northern Ireland.[15]

The Northern Irish government remained officially neutral in the matter due to the large number of alternative relief bodies, which could do as they wished once they abided by the law. The government was willing to facilitate any transferral of southern Protestants to the North, including the exchange of farmlands between Free State Loyalists and Northern Irish Nationalists.[16] These relief projects were important for Ulster Unionists for two purposes: to consolidate Unionist and Protestant dominance in Northern Ireland, and to rescue southern Protestants on the verge of bankruptcy and from harassment.[17] The UUC reported receiving many letters from Protestants across the Free State, detailing their plights and pleading for help. T.F. Stewart and Rowley Elliott, UUP MP for South Tyrone, even made an offer while at a meeting of the Caledon Branch of the South Tyrone Women's Unionist Association to provide free furniture vans to any Northern Irish Catholics who wished to emigrate to the Free State.[18] This was in hopes of giving a further financial incentive to make such a transfer scheme work. They, of course, felt deep sympathy for their counterparts in Southern Ireland, that later became the Irish Free State. However, the transferral scheme had a crucial flaw; Stormont received no applications from Northern Irish Nationalists wishing to exchange their farmlands and emigrate to the Irish Free State, causing much disappointment among Loyalists north and south of the border.[19] The government could not interfere without mutual consent, despite the degree of discrimination Catholics faced, from employment and housing to gerrymandered elections in Northern Ireland, providing a constant reinforcement of motivation to emigrate.[20] An unnamed speaker behind the Memorial, who matched James Fleming's description as an extensive landowner in Donegal who lived near St Johnston and a well-known member of the local Orange Order, spoke to the *Irish Times* concerning this by explaining:

I know at least twenty farmers in this neighbourhood who
would only be too happy to exchange holdings with dissatisfied
Nationalists in Northern Ireland, but I am certain that any
Nationalist who has a good farm there will prefer to stay where
he is.[21]

Another reaction to the issue was an allegation made by a cross-
channel Catholic publication that the East Donegal Memorial was
engineered in Belfast. They claimed the Memorial was never meant
to be successful as the petition's true purpose was to eventually lead to
a mass population exchange between several thousand Northern Irish
Catholics for southern Irish Protestants. Some of the Nationalist press
went further, comparing the scheme as a new Ulster Plantation. Sir
William Hungerford, who was mentioned in the article for helping
establish a fund for southern Protestants to buy Northern Irish
farmlands, denied the accusations. He claimed they were without
foundation, as the Northern government maintained impartiality by
treating Protestants and Catholics equally. All were welcomed by the
Northern Irish government to reside in the state, who wished to live
in peace and work for the benefit of the state. He admitted that 'it is
the people who fight against, and work for the downfall of, the Ulster
government who are naturally not encouraged here'.[22] Some did not
consider any such transferral scheme to be serious, with McManus
believing it was another propaganda stunt. Even if it was possible, he
believed it would be unwise from a police point of view as it could
cause some local unrest.[23]

The Memorial and how to respond to the Donegal Loyalists were
still being discussed by the Stormont cabinet on 5 March 1935.[24]
On 25 February 1935 the press reported 'sensational developments'
concerning the Memorial, as two suspected agents were seen in east
Donegal making investigations. Inspired by these press reports, the
Gardaí investigated this potential development, which later proved
to be a mistaken report. The Gardaí found the two men in question;
they were interrogated and found to be Englishmen Thomas Webb,
from Bedford, and William Emery, from Northampton. They were
travelling the area with their bicycles distributing free bibles on behalf
of the International Bible Students' Society, London, and asking for
subscriptions to help cover the costs of production and distribution

of their bibles. McManus believed the men were 'little better than vagrants', but they had no connection with the Memorialists.[25] The *Londonderry Sentinel* used the occasion to once again belittle and criticize the *Derry Journal*'s reporting of 'sensational developments' concerning the East Donegal Memorial which turned out to be untrue, to which the *Journal* never responded.[26]

Despite no further incidents, the Gardaí kept the file open until 1937.[27] The Memorial remained a heated political topic, as it was a public challenge to the Fianna Fáil government, criticizing community relations in the Free State and highlighting that the Economic War they started was not going well. On 18 November, just a few days after the Memorial was announced, a meeting was held for the delegates of the East and South Donegal Blueshirts in Ballybofey. Patrick Belton, TD for Dublin North, used the meeting to announce General O'Duffy's intention to establish his own political party following his recent split with Fine Gael.[28] Whether the meeting was perfectly timed in terms of dates, or purposely used the political dissent the Memorial had generated in the county, is unknown. Either way, the Memorial was certainly used to their advantage, to show a new style of politics was perhaps needed in order to resolve some of the issues Fianna Fáil had created.

A few months later on 7 January 1935, James Dillon, Fine Gael TD for Donegal, spoke at Kilsaran, Co. Louth. He discussed the Anglo-Irish trade war and how it was damaging the Free State economy, with the recent offer of exchange of populations with Northern Ireland as a key demonstration of the state of the national economy. Dillon argued 'it is hardly a tribute to the Free State government that when the offer of exchange of Nationalists from the North for Unionists in east Donegal was made not a single Nationalist in the Six Counties availed of it'.[29] The Free State government needed to address this situation before it started making the Irish public question their ability to govern. A few months later on 3 March, the minister for lands, Joseph Connolly, spoke at an annual Fianna Fáil meeting at John Colgan Hall in Carndonagh. He used the opportunity to dismiss the Memorial's claims of religious intolerance in the Free State, and tried to turn the situation in their favour, that the fault was due to partition:

In this border county and the 'Six County' border counties
adjoining it, the tragedy of Partition is more clearly brought
home to one than any part of Ireland. We have the great port
of Derry – and remember, Derry is an Irish city – cut off from
its natural markets in Tirconaill and the interchange of labour,
trade and social life interrupted, and by whom – not by the
people of Derry, not by any decision of the Irish people, but
by the political manipulations of certain statesmen who felt
and feel that the security of empire can only be maintained by
division between our people.

We have recently heard of certain interested parties who
endeavour by memorial and petition to protest against being
cut off from what they call their 'Loyalist' friends across the
border ... I would also like to stress the fact that it is my anxious
desire to see secured the re-union of all our people, irrespective
of creed or class, in a complete and unified Irish nation ... Go
through any part of the Free State with its ninety-three per cent
population of one religion, and you will find no intolerance,
no barriers to equal rights and equal opportunity for the seven
per cent minority. That is as it should be in a normal healthy
Ireland.[30]

The minister's claim would be proven wrong, just two months
later. In east Donegal there were a series of celebrations for the
king's silver jubilee on 6 May. In Raphoe, the largest bonfire in the
county took place on a hill above the town and acted as a signal for
many other smaller bonfires to be set alight, and fifty other bonfires
were reported to have been lit in east Donegal. The Lifford Orange
Lodge pipe band even crossed the border to be part of a celebration
parade with the local lodge in Strabane, along with contingents
from Artigarvan, Bready and Donemana.[31] Nonetheless, not all of
these celebrations went off without incident. At a bonfire at Binion
Hill, near St Johnston, a group of two hundred loyalists celebrated
the jubilee until shots were fired in the direction of the bonfire, with
reports differing from just a few to a hundred, yet no one was injured.
As two men armed with revolvers approached the bonfire, with one
witness account claiming they were part of an eight-man party,
they demanded to know who was in charge of the bonfire. A young

man named Robert Long, son of the individual that lit the bonfire, stepped forward and claimed responsibility. He was ordered to put his hands up, which he refused to do, telling the assailants to shoot if they wished. The men decided to leave, most likely in fear the crowd would follow Long's example and go against them, as the group continued their celebrations and made three cheers to the king. Two men were arrested, but were released by the morning of the following day.[32] That day news of the incident became widespread, being reported in the local and national press across Ireland and parts of England.[33] It nevertheless failed to dampen the spirits of the Donegal Loyalists. During the Orange Order's Twelfth of July demonstration in Derry/Londonderry, the city's parade saw the largest contingent of Donegal Orangemen ever to take part. Both the celebrations and their record turnout were demonstrations of their belief and resolve that they belonged in Northern Ireland.[34]

The bonfire shooting would not be an isolated incident that year. A few days following the Twelfth, a series of attacks on Protestant businesses occurred in Letterkenny in the early hours of 16 July. Windows of five shops in the town that were owned by Protestants were smashed by stones. During the incident, the Donegal Service Depot, owned by John Buchanan of Strabane and serving an extensive area of the county, was set alight. The fire destroyed the garage, one lorry, four cars and much of the depot's equipment. The cost of the fire damage represented a loss of £10,000, and a potential loss of employment for sixteen men. If it were not for the help from local residents, the Gardaí and firefighters, the extent of the damage would have been much worse. They were able to save one lorry, eight cars, some of the machinery and parts, which gave the Buchanans' company hope they could make temporary plans that would allow for business to continue.[35] This attack was not directed towards the Memorialists, but as a repercussion for sectarian riots in Belfast that began during the Twelfth and continued afterwards. The Catholic community suffered greatly. By 20 July, the riots had resulted in 5 deaths, over 50 houses burned out or damaged, 100 people injured with 70 in hospital.[36] By the end of the month, there were reports that up to 384 families were evicted, affecting 1,646 people, and many others were afraid to go to work or leave their homes in fear of further violence.[37] The attack in Letterkenny was part of a number of other attacks targeting Protestants across the Free State during the rest of July that year, as a number of Catholics desired revenge for the incidents that took place in Belfast. Several Protestant-owned properties were burned down or damaged, including four cottages near Arva, Co. Cavan; a Protestant church in Kilmallock, Co. Limerick; two Protestant halls and a hall of the local Masonic order in Clones, Co. Monaghan, along with many other incidents in the rest of the country. The situation got very serious, as the Gardaí started guarding Protestant churches and streets.[38] There were calls from Galway dock workers for local Protestants to be dismissed from their employment, and similar calls were made in Sligo, Limerick and Waterford. This was a dark period of violence across Ireland, even with Garda protection.[39]

Both the Memorial and these attacks on Free State Protestants became a source of propaganda against the Irish Free State for the Northern Irish government. Hugh MacDowell Pollock, minister of finance for Northern Ireland, spoke at an annual meeting of the Windsor Unionist Association on 21 March 1935. He used the opportunity to respond to recent calls for a united Ireland, made by local Nationalist politicians during St Patrick's Day. He reminded those present of the East Donegal Memorialists, which showed the hard economic conditions these dairy farmers were enduring in the Free State, leading some to desire to be on the Northern Irish side of the border. This, he argued, should make them thank God for their blessings that they were British citizens.[40] Nevertheless, the Memorial became an issue for some six-county Unionists to criticize Lord Craigavon's government. On 1 January 1935, the Derry branch of the Ulster Protestant League held a highly attended meeting at the Derry Guildhall, including over a hundred people from Belfast. The league was an extreme Loyalist organization with anti-Catholic objectives, including purging the police force, post office and all government departments in Northern Ireland of 'all disloyal traitors who infest them'. The organization was considered so extreme that the RUC placed a shorthand note-taker from Belfast at the meeting to take notes, and most local Ulster Unionist politicians did not wish to be associated with it. However, they sent apology letters, that they could not attend, in order to save face, as they still required their members support. This included high-profile figures, such as the minister of

Agriculture for Northern Ireland, the mayor of Derry/Londonderry, the city high sheriff, and the MP for the city of Londonderry in the parliament of Northern Ireland. The Londonderry Protestant League secretary, G.W. Smyth, let it be known they backed Craigavon's government. This support was conditional nevertheless, for as long as the government maintained the principle of a Protestant parliament for a Protestant people, and free of self-serving politicians. There was an element of mistrust of the local Unionist leadership. James Gallagher, a local councillor, spoke at the meeting. He let it be known there were 'Lundies and traitors' in their midst, and they were sick of the policy adopted by their local leaders in Derry/Londonderry, believing they were Unionists in name only. Gallagher accused them of rarely giving any financial assistance to Protestants in distress, yet continuing to donate to the St Vincent de Paul Society and Nazareth House. Furthermore, the vice-chairman of the league, McConnell, stated to those present that the position of east Donegal Loyalists needed to be looked into.[41]

Many months later another well-attended league meeting was held on 9 October in the Ulster Hall, Belfast. The league's anger towards the Northern Irish government had grown, and they passed two resolutions. The first protested Craigavon's speech at Bessbrook for promising to protect the Catholic minority; the second demanded the resignations of Bates as minister of home affairs, and Sir Charles Wickham as general inspector of the Royal Ulster Constabulary.[42] Their agenda served the interests of the Donegal Unionists, and one of the speakers at the meeting was Revd Alexander Thornton McEvoy, a Presbyterian minister from St Johnston. He was believed to be originally from Lisburn and had served in the British Army at one point. He had moved to St Johnston with his wife and family in 1930, with rumours that he was not a properly ordained clergyman and was a 'street preacher' prior to moving to the area. Before the league meeting, he had attended Orange demonstrations within Northern Ireland and had spoken at a meeting within the six counties, of religious intolerance within the Free State, a few years prior.[43] At the league meeting, McEvoy reminded the audience that during the Home Rule movement when Sir Edward Carson inspected the Donegal UVF in Raphoe they were told that the Ulster counties of Cavan, Donegal and Monaghan would never be put under the

authority of a Dublin government. That promise was not kept, and
because of this Donegal Loyalists were under a government that had
no sympathy towards them. They had been singled out for persecution
and harassment. He then asked all those present to put into power
a government that would bring the Donegal Loyalists back with the
rest of Northern Ireland, and save them from the persecution and
suffering they were enduring in the Free State. McEvoy then asked
all those present to stand (which they did) and take an oath to 'see the
people of east Donegal through in their struggle'.[44]

This speech initially suggests that both he and potentially other
members of the Presbyterian, Church of Ireland or Methodist clergy
within east Donegal either supported the Memorial or were part of
the campaign. McEvoy, nevertheless, was not exactly who he seemed.
Following the league meeting, and press reporting of McEvoy's
speech, the Gardaí took an interest in both the meeting and the speaker
from 11 December. They were concerned that his statements would
have an effect in disrupting community relations in east Donegal
and encourage developments for the Memorialist campaign. On 15
December, a report was written on his background and status within
east Donegal. He had very little influence, as his church in St Johnston
was described as a 'tin hut' with a congregation of twelve persons
from four families. He was tolerated by both religions in east Donegal
because while Catholics ignored him Protestants primarily accepted
him simply because 'he was not a papist'. He was seen as someone
trying to gain recognition and a reputation of public standing in the
Protestant community in order to obtain a promotion to a wealthier
parish in Northern Ireland than his current position in St Johnston,
which had a remuneration of just £1 per week. The Gardaí suspected
this was why he took an active role in the Protestant League and tried
to hijack the Memorialist campaign; it is unknown if he truly was
involved with the movement. Despite this, McManus was concerned
his speech in Belfast had angered the Catholic community in east
Donegal, particularly in St Johnston, and believed that the Gardaí
may need to take measures to prevent any 'illegal action' being carried
out upon him.[45]

4. Derry–Donegal Milk War

The Memorial successfully raised awareness of and sympathy for east Donegal Protestants across the British Empire yet failed to resolve the Northern Ireland Milk Act's impact on Donegal. The Donegal dairy farmers who decided to remain were given a reprieve. The Milk Act was meant to come into force on 16 December, but Donegal milk vendors entered Derry/Londonderry with their goods as usual the following day. They had received letters from the Ministry of Agriculture for Northern Ireland, stating they could continue to supply their products until further notice.[1] This was due to the press coverage concerning the east Donegal farmers, and several Unionist politicians and institutions calling for support. Matthew Kerr, as well as other contacts the Memorialists utilized, was instrumental in this undertaking. Through positions they held, resolutions were sent to Stormont by the City of Derry Grand Orange Lodge on 16 November and the council of the City of Londonderry and Foyle Unionist Association on 30 October and 13 December 1934, respectively.[2]

The reprieve the Donegal Milk vendors gained was only temporary, as the Northern Irish government now felt pressure from farmers in Co. Londonderry. When the Milk Act was introduced, the Derry Milk Vendors Association originally passed a resolution that called upon the government of Northern Ireland to include farmers within Donegal under the scheme. They later stated they passed the resolution to show their sympathies with their counterparts, as they believed the government would not make such an exemption.[3] The association sent representatives to the Ministry of Agriculture to stop the supply of milk from Donegal. When this failed, the association decided to be open with their intentions and, on 6 January, passed a resolution calling on the Northern Irish government to exclude the Donegal dairy farmers. A few days later, on 10 January, they sent a deputation to the ministry to urge that the Milk Act be enforced against these farmers.[4] This antagonism towards the Donegal farmers was as a result of them selling their milk at a much lower price than the price fixed for dairy suppliers from Northern Ireland.[5] New milk suppliers from Co. Londonderry started to enter the city hoping to replace the Donegal farmers' trade.[6] Instead, supply far exceeded demand and led to a situation in which the Northern Irish suppliers were coming away from the market every day with twenty to thirty gallons of unsold milk.[7] The police did not interfere with the Donegal farmers, besides give warnings they were open to prosecutions without a licence and took the names of all milk vendors from the Free State selling their goods in the city. Despite these threats, the Donegal farmers continued to go over the border to trade their goods.[8]

This series of stand-offs and threats became known as the 'Derry–Donegal Milk War'. During this period, people in Co. Londonderry favoured the Laggan Valley farmers on account of their traditional ties to the region and sympathy for them, being bitterly betrayed again by those in Northern Ireland.[9] Myles became the official representative of the Donegal dairy farmers during the crisis.[10] He tried to reach an agreement with the backing of both the Donegal farmers and the Free State government. These efforts ranged from visiting Stormont on 5 and 11 January to talk with Basil Brooke, to making public appeals to the people of Northern Ireland for an extension of a few months to allow a transition period, all of which were in vain.[11] Joseph Alexander and Thomas Boyd Rankin were confirmed to appear at Stormont, prior to all this, on 13 December, though it is unknown who they met or if they even had a scheduled appointment with anyone at Stormont. The Gardaí believed Scott and Myles were with them, but this may have been a mistake. There was a constant suspicion by the Gardaí that Scott and Myles were involved with the Memorial or stirring up the Donegal milk vendors in some manner throughout this period; and the Gardaí made continuous efforts to obtain evidence to prove their suspicions.[12]

The 'Milk War' came to a brief halt by 18 January when it came up in Belfast's King's Bench Division. A farmer, Joseph Alexander, lived in Derry/Londonderry and had a farm in Imlick, Co. Donegal; when he applied for a licence, he was initially denied due to the location of his farm. When he took this to court, his solicitor pointed out that section 2 (sub-section 2) of the Milk Act was vague, as the act stated that 'any person' could apply for a licence; the lord chief justice himself questioned 'Could this include a Frenchman?'

Alexander's solicitor pointed out that under the act there was not a single reference to the Irish Free State or to the status of the person applying for a licence, who in this case was a British subject like many Donegal farmers. Thus, there was nothing to prevent his client from obtaining a licence. The court ruled that as Stormont was a devolved institution, the Northern Irish government and its ministries could not implement acts that affected trade between different parts of the British Empire, as this power was reserved to Westminster; therefore, the act could not be legally enforced.[13] This was later overturned in the Belfast Court of Appeal. The Northern Irish government could not give milk licences in areas outside their control, and the Donegal milk vendors were warned to stop selling their produce by 23 June or face the threat of prosecution. This convinced the Donegal farmers to make an appeal to the British House of Lords asking if they could apply for milk licences.[14] The ban deeply hurt and troubled the loyalists of east Donegal, which continued for several years, and their anger was reflected during the Twelfth of 1936. The Orangemen of east Donegal, which fell under the jurisdiction of the City of Derry Grand Orange Lodge, decided not to join their demonstration that year. Instead, they joined their counterparts in south Donegal to hold their demonstration in Rossnowlagh, the first time this had been done in many years.[15] When the House of Lords finally heard the appeal it was September 1937, and while they sympathized with the farmers they upheld the decision that the Northern Irish Ministry of Agriculture did not have the power to grant licences to producers that resided outside its territorial boundaries.[16]

By December 1937, as a measure to help the economic condition in north-east Donegal, plans were made to establish a new bacon-curing factory in Donegal. As an alternative new industry for the lost milk trade, it was backed by a substantial grant from the Free State government. The proposals caused a rivalry between the towns of Carndonagh and Letterkenny over the location of the factory.[17] The decision took years, and the rivalry intensified through local fundraising. This was because one of the conditions of the selection process for the proposed location of the new factory would be based on funds raised by the local community. Inishowen farmers raised £7,000 for a factory in Carndonagh and Laggan farmers raised £15,000 for a factory in Letterkenny or Ramelton by August 1939.[18]

Letterkenny was chosen as the factory site by February 1940 and went into operation in November.[19] The Irish government also built two alcohol factories in Carndonagh and Manorcunningham to encourage local farmers to grow potatoes. But even when they were established by 1937 there were claims from Fine Gael senator John McLoughlin that these factories did not fully help farmers. The managing director of the alcohol factory was receiving £1,800 per year while farmers were receiving £2 per ton of potatoes, showing who was benefitting the most from this system.[20]

The East Donegal Orange Order decided to make a last-ditch effort to save the milk trade and end the ban by publishing a resolution in the December 1937 half-yearly report of the Grand Orange Lodge of Ireland. In the resolution, they wanted to draw the attention of members of the Orange Order to the hardships created by the ban on milk entering Northern Ireland from the Irish Free State, and they appealed to the members of the Northern Ireland cabinet to introduce an amending bill as soon as possible to alleviate this. They hoped that such a heartfelt resolution would make their Orange brethren in the six counties, as well as the Ulster Unionist leaders within the order, understand how the milk ban was impacting their Protestant community (appendix 6). They described their hardships, their contributions in the First World War and helping to establish the state of Northern Ireland, and used anti-Catholic language to provoke a reaction from some hardline zealous Orangemen. For example, the final line of their resolution declared 'surely our Orange brethren in the Six Counties will not willingly see Free State Orangemen victimised to make way for Six County Roman Catholic disloyalists?'[21] This was written despite the fact that the majority of east Donegal Protestants had good relations with their Catholic neighbours, showing an element of desperation to get as much sympathy as possible for their plight.

The Milk War came to an end in June 1938 when a new Milk and Milk Products Bill was passed in Stormont, which allowed east Donegal dairy farmers to supply milk to the city of Derry/Londonderry; this was partly due to need as well, as plans were announced for a new milk factory in the city, which would require the produce of the east Donegal milk vendors. The mayor of the Maiden City, Sir James McElmunn Wilton, expressed his satisfaction with the amendment.[22]

Conclusion

The East Donegal Memorial and the Milk War that followed could be regarded as post-partition aftershocks within southern Irish Unionism, as people adjusted to life outside the UK. Feeling besieged, conservative elements within the Protestant community adopted a 'No Surrender' mentality as they reacted to defy the legal and political changes in Ireland that further distanced them from their ancestral roots and their identified homeland and heritage. Donegal Unionists and German Loyalists in Upper Silesia during the 1920s and 1930s both had a strong sense of irredentism, to repeal an unjust wrong; however, the Polish border was determined and enforced upon Germany by the Allied nations through the Treaty of Versailles. Nevertheless, Germans in Poland had support from the German government for the reincorporation of their area into Germany. While the Irish border was determined by both the British government and the UUC opting for a six-county exclusion, when these Donegal irredentists campaigned to rectify this they found their answer was silence from those who had abandoned them again, despite their proven loyalty.[1]

The Memorial may have failed in its objective to alter the Irish boundary line, but it did raise the profile of the situation for east Donegal Protestants and sympathy for their plight in Northern Ireland, Great Britain and the wider British Empire. Other southern Unionist petitions were made since that period, but not as such serious movements. On 19 March 2002 a 'Liberate Donegal' online petition was launched, calling for Donegal's incorporation into Northern Ireland. This was established eighty years after the creation of the Irish border and sixty-eight years since the 1934 Memorials. This Unionist petition remained active up to January 2019 and had been viewed 2,767 times since its launch but nevertheless received only five signatures worldwide after seventeen years of existence. This small signature count could reflect the low support for neo-Unionism, a technological gap for senior citizens or an absence of advertisement to make people aware of the existence of the petition, while others may have found locating the petition an arduous task. It is primarily because the petition was never a genuine political action, however, as the last line of the petition was written for humour:

> We, the undersigned, call on the government of the Republic of Ireland to free the people of Donegal from their suffering by immediately taking action to hand Donegal over to the government of the UK, so that Donegal will become part of Northern Ireland. Note that this petition only calls for action re the county of Donegal. The people of Northern Ireland do not want County Monaghan because it is full of troublemakers.[2]

This could be compared to another online petition that was launched in 2015 demanding an Irish referendum in 2020 for the Republic of Ireland to re-unify with the UK, which obtained just 95 signatures and was created by Orin Mhando, an American citizen in Waterbury, Connecticut.[3] The petition, despite its low support, was evaluated by the Irish Joint Committee on Public Petitions. It was examined for compliance with standing orders on 4 August and 4 November 2015, before being considered on 4 November 2015 by the committee, which ruled it as non-admissible.[4] Another petition was submitted on 29 November 2019 to the UK government and parliament, titled 'Invite Co. Donegal to re-join the United Kingdom'. The petitioners argued the county shares a longer border with Northern Ireland than with the rest of the Republic of Ireland, and the county was part of the same province of Ulster as the six counties of Northern Ireland. The petition received no signatures, as it was initially rejected due to the fact that it did not meet petition standards, because this was a matter for the people of Co. Donegal and the government of the Republic of Ireland, not the British government.[5] No southern Unionist petition ever received the same momentum and caught the attention of the press as the 1934 Memorial of east Donegal did. Documents, letters and newspaper cuttings concerning the Memorial and the Derry–Donegal Milk War held at PRONI were released to the public in 1978, causing a small stir of curiosity in the local press in Derry/Londonderry and Co. Donegal.[6]

The memory of the Milk War has devolved into local folklore in Donegal, more than the Memorial has, due to how long the Economic

War went on for and the number of livelihoods that were ruined during this period; but both events have influenced some works of literature. A prime example can be seen within Kenneth Dodds' *Donegal–Fermanagh series*, concerning a Presbyterian family from east Donegal called the Vances as they adapt to political challenges they face from 1895 to 1957. In his book *The demons of discord* he dedicates three chapters to the Memorial. In this work the Memorial was organized through a 'Petition Committee', described as a shadowy inner core within the east Donegal Association (CDPRA). Dodd even writes scenes of how these events affect relations between certain characters that take opposing views of the petition. Jamie Vance has an argument with his boss, Henry Forbes, the manager of the Donegal Railway Company. While they were both members of the 'EDA' Forbes was a member of the committee and even admits he was responsible for some of the text of the Memorial, which Jamie feels would cause more problems than it would potentially solve. Following this confrontation, and seeing his Protestant neighbours in fear of repercussions, Jamie feels disillusioned with the EDA and eventually decides to resign from the association entirely. Another scene is of an emergency meeting of the local Donegal IRA cell on 14 November, concerning how they should react to the Memorial. Numerous suggestions come forward. These range from getting the names of the leaders of the Memorialists and destroying their farms; finding out more information first with gentle enquiries before deciding upon any action, and finally a staged approach, getting a local Nationalist leader in a position of authority to condemn the Memorialists, and if they continue then use heavy-handed tactics. A member of the cell, Danny Wall, then states 'I'm off to pay a visit to my new friend in Letterkenny'. The scene then ends, and the 'friend in Letterkenny' is hinted to be District Justice Louis Walsh. The next scene is him making his statement to the press at Letterkenny Court the following day, with the reporters joking with each other as he makes his speech: 'thinks he's in the Garda now!' or 'Is he usually like this? He thinks he's the Minister of Defence now!'[7] These scenes that Dodd wrote are a work of pure fiction, drama to entertain the reader and not based on any truth. Nevertheless, when historians do not have all the information, works of literature begin to flourish in the gaps made by unanswerable questions to fill the void of the unknown, and a work like *The demons of discord* is no different. Was there an official 'Petition Committee' of some kind? Did the IRA feel some concern towards the Memorialists or commit any action against them, such as the bonfire shootings? What did reporters initially think, or how did they react, when Walsh made his statement? These questions, as well as many others, may forever remain unanswered.

Nearly a century after the Memorial the event is recognized as a key part of the local heritage of the Protestant and Ulster-Scots community in Co. Donegal. In 2013, the Ulster-Scots Community Network wrote a short history of the Ulster Plantation in the county, recognizing the 1934 Memorial as an element of this legacy.[8]

Draft Memorial, June 1934

We, the undersigned, representing 5,000 Loyalists in east Donegal and the Lagan [sic] District, present this MEMORIAL to you, the Members of His Majesty's Imperial government and the government of Northern Ireland, praying you to restore to us our former rights and liberties, by placing us under His Majesty's government in Northern Ireland.

Many of us have been and are being threatened daily with violence and told that we shall be riddled with bullets at the first opportunity. When threats of this nature are reported to the Civic Guard we are told that they are unable to take any action. We feel that our lives and property are in danger under the Free State government.

We are cut off from our Market Towns (Londonderry, Strabane and Belfast), and we find it almost impossible to exist. We do not know what steps the Free State government may take in the near future to further harass and impoverish us. The confiscation of our property and, perhaps, the taking of our lives are ever present possibilities.

Impartiality and fairness in the issue of Cattle Export Licences do not exist. Many Loyalists who, in the year 1933, exported up to 80 head of cattle have been told that they are not recognized as having exported any cattle during that year and licences are refused them, whereas Fianna Fáil supporters get all the licences they require. Thus, this regulation which was passed by His Majesty's Imperial government is used as a weapon against those who are loyal to the imperial connection.

Recently the Free State government have granted licences to their supporters to fish the water of the River Foyle, regardless of the rights of the owners of this fishery. At the present time many of these supporters are actually engaged in fishing operations.

We feel that our land and property may similarly be filched from us.

We pay 85 per cent of the entire rates of County Donegal and we have no say in the expenditure of these rates. We own 90 per cent of the property in this area and we constitute at 75 per cent of the population.

We would most strongly impress upon you that we belong to the Imperial Province of Ulster. That we, with 30,000 other Loyalists of Donegal, were signatories of Ulster's Solemn League & Covenant, and that, in spite of this Solemn Covenant, we were cut off from our fellow Loyalists in the Six Counties, under the treaty. We successfully fought our case for inclusion in the Six Counties before the Border Commission, but the report of this commission was never adopted.

Under the treaty certain rights were assured to us for our protection, such as the right of Appeal to His Majesty's Privy Council. These rights have been taken from us by the action of the Free State government, and our last remaining protection 'the Seanad' is about to be dissolved.

Under the Free State Land Act of 1933 our title to our farms has been taken from us.

Your Memorialists pray that you will consider our plight and will send us a message of hope that the findings of Judge Feetham's Commission will be put in force. Otherwise, there is nothing for us but to come out of the Free State and to relinquish our homes and all that we hold dear.

We assure His Majesty's government of Northern Ireland that if our petition is granted, we shall be loyal subjects as we were in former and happier times.

Signed on behalf of 5,000 loyal Protestants of this area.

First Memorial, 14 November 1934

The humble petition of 7,368 loyal subjects of the king residing in east Donegal and the Lagan [*sic*] District of the county, sheweth –

We whose names are subscribed on behalf of ourselves and our families, humbly pray that His Imperial Majesty's government, being a party to the Anglo-Irish Treaty of 1921, will take steps to restore us to our former rights and liberties by placing us under His Majesty's government in Northern Ireland.

We feel that our lives and property are not secure under the Free State government. We are cut off from our market towns – Londonderry, Strabane and Belfast – and we find it almost impossible to exist. We do not know what steps the Free State government may take in the near future to further harass and impoverish us. The confiscation of our property and, perhaps, the taking of our lives, are ever present possibilities.

Impartiality and fairness in the issue of cattle export licences do not exist. Fianna Fáil supporters get all the licences they require, whereas many loyal Protestants have been refused point blank and told that they are not recognized as having exported any cattle in 1933, although many of them had exported over 80 head.

Recently the Free State government have granted licences to their supporters to fish the waters of the River Foyle, regardless of the rights of the owners of this fishery. At the present time many of these supporters are actually engaged in fishing operations.

We feel that our land and property may similarly be filched from us. In the Laggan area of the County Donegal we pay 85% of the rates and we have no say in the expenditure of these rates. We own 90% of the land and property in that area and we constitute at least 75%

of the population. In the same area there are 23 Protestant places of worship as against 6 Roman Catholic churches.

We would most strongly impress upon H.M. imperial government that we belong to the Imperial Province of Ulster; that we, with 30,000 other Loyalists of Donegal, were signatories of Ulster's Solemn League & Covenant, and that, in spite of this Solemn Covenant, we were cut off from our fellow Loyalists in the Six Counties under the treaty. We successfully fought our case for inclusion in the Six Counties before the Border Commission, but the report was never adopted.

Under the treaty certain rights were assured to us for our protection, such as the right of Appeal to the Privy Council. These rights have been taken from us by the action of the Free State government, and our last remaining protection 'the Seanad' is about to be dissolved.

Under the Free State Land Act of 1933 our title to our farms has been taken from us. Unless the findings of Judge Feetham's Commission are put in force, there will be nothing for us but to come out from the Free State and to relinquish our homes and all that we hold most dear.

YOUR PETITIONERS THEREFORE HUMBLY PRAY that His Majesty's Imperial government will consider our plight and take such steps as may be in their power for the protection of ourselves and our property and the upholding of our rights and liberties as British subjects so that we may be able to continue loyal subjects of the king as in former and happier times.

AND YOUR PETITIONERS WILL EVER PRAY.

Second Memorial, 29 November 1934

Since WE, THE LOYALISTS OF EAST DONEGAL AND THE LAGGAN DISTRICT, sent our memorial to his Majesty's government at Westminster and his Majesty's government of Northern Ireland our position has become more critical.

Recent legislation in the Irish Free State prohibiting the importation of potatoes into Northern Ireland, the Northern Ireland milk scheme, which will come into operation soon, and the Irish Free State Beef Bill leave us without any market for our produce, and we are absolutely unable to meet the demands on us.

Many of us have paid our land annuities twice over, some of us three times, in tariffs, as we can prove by receipts, and we have to pay half land annuities to the Irish Free State government. If we cannot pay, bailiffs are sent to seize our stock without giving us an opportunity of explaining our position in court.

Recent newspaper reports say Mr de Valera's government can and will declare a Republic and make us foreigners and aliens in the British Commonwealth, of which we have always been loyal citizens, and where many of our friends and relations have found homes.

Under the Irish Free State Citizenship Bill he seeks to deprive us of our status as British subjects.

Our children are compelled to learn Irish in school. It is of no commercial value, and it is a handicap to them in competitive examinations for positions in the British Commonwealth.

During the civil war and after we did our best as loyal citizens of the Irish Free State, and in the last two or three years of Mr Cosgrave's government we had hopes that our efforts would be rewarded. We have now reluctantly to admit that we are on the verge of bankruptcy and ruin.

We, the Loyalists of east Donegal and Laggan district therefore pray His Majesty's government, if our area is not transferred to Northern Ireland, to appoint a commission to inquire into our present state of affairs and transfer those who wish to farms of equal valuation in Northern Ireland or England and dissatisfied Nationalists in Northern Ireland to the Irish Free State.

His Majesty's government has assisted in transferring Jews to Palestine and rectifying borders or boundaries abroad, and we trust, therefore, that they will grant the prayer of this memorial.

District Justice Louis Joseph Walsh statement, 15 November 1934

I have no concern with the political considerations involved, but as this court is primarily responsible for good order in the area, I am very much concerned about the threat of its peace which the circulation of this document entails, and it is only my duty to see that all attempts at treasonable activities should be repressed.

I refer to a petition which is being carried round for a signature which contains several scandalous and utterly groundless statements about the government and the administration of Saorstát *Éireann*, and which seeks the intervention of some outside authority in order to detach from the Saorstát portion of the territory solemnly guaranteed to it by a document internationally recognized and registered by the League of Nations.

It is only because that the abnormal frame of mind bred in us by years of oppression has confused our manner of thinking that those who are being foolish enough to sign this petition have not adverted to its illegality and treasonable nature.

What would happen to a Frenchman who hawked a document through Alsace making slanderous statements about the French administration in the province and seeking to have it transferred to Germany, or what would happen if a body of Englishmen conspired to have Cornwall handed over to France?

The sooner that our citizens realize that ours is a Sovereign state that will not permit any encroachment of its rights the better it will be for everybody.

I therefore desire to warn those who have had anything to do with this document that they have been engaged in a treasonable practice. Probably many of them have acted in ignorance, and as I would be sorry to see the drastic provision of the Public Safety Act applied to people who are in the main good citizens and who have been induced to sign this document under pressure from designing outsiders and without full advertence to its implication, I trust this warning will be sufficient and restrain them from any further illegalities. This petition is, however, worse than a crime on the part of those responsible for it. It is a blunder.

It is well known that the Tory cabinet which had to deal with the Feetham report was prevented from interfering with the Donegal border by the confidential reports received from trustworthy sources.

In Ireland feeling ran so high as the result of the threat to the integrity of this county that for some weeks we all sat on a powder barrel. Any attempt to transfer even a townland of Donegal would have provoked a series of fights, burnings and reprisals on both sides of the Border and led to conflagration, the end of which no man could have foreseen.

The British Cabinet considered the matter carefully and decided they were not going to risk a renewal of hostilities in Ireland for the sake of a few anti-Irish bigots in St Johnston or Burt.

We do not want a recurrence of the high feeling of that time, and any attempt to provoke it must be regarded as a serious menace to the peace of the district, the disturbance of which could only result in very serious loss upon the people of Donegal who are most active in the matter. The risk is one hundred times greater now because our present cabinet is one which knows its own mind, and has never been afraid to stand for its full rights.

The object of these petitioners can only be achieved by action on the part of the British government, and we all know any attempt to filch even a sod of Donegal from the Free State would result in the national army being marched to the border. It might only be a small army, but it could, at least, resist long enough to fire a mine which might throw all Europe into horrors of war.

The Free State is a member of the League of Nations. The important world seats are represented by ambassadors in Dublin. England has signed the Kellogg and other peace pacts and a shot fired anywhere from the Balkans to Newtowncunningham might unloose the dogs of war over Europe. Does any sane man, therefore, think that astute English statesmen are going to risk all this for the sake of a few gallons of milk from Laggan (Donegal).

Therefore, Donegal Unionists should make up their minds to keep clear of fooleries of this sort, which are principally engineered from outside sources. Their interests are now identical with ours and their best policy is to accept things as they find them and settle down as good and loyal citizens of the state.

As a matter of fact, most of them were prepared to do so, but were only prevented from saying it openly by the want of moral courage, which had always been noticeable in Ulster, and by the unfair pressure being applied to them by designing political propagandists.

There are Protestant families, I believe, who say privately that they are doing quite well under the new conditions, but who are afraid to admit it publicly.

Failure of moral courage is, however, not illegal, and it is no concern of this court, but to put one's name to a slanderous document is quite another matter, in regard to which I think it my duty to utter this warning.

This court is not concerned with anyone's politics, but if anything is being done which in my opinion tends to provoke attacks on the public peace or weaken the respect of lawful authority, I will always look upon it as my duty to warn people against it.

Letter to the *Irish Times* editor by District Justice Louis Joseph Walsh, 29 November 1934

SIR, – In your leading article of Saturday you suggest that I was in error in attributing illegality to those people who were going round my court district endeavouring to induce farmers and others to sign a petition requesting 'His Majesty's government in Northern Ireland' to accept them as 'loyal subjects'.

You appear, however, to have confused the issue, and it may be worth while to make clear wherein lay the offence of which I complained. Anybody is, and should be, quite free to preach in public that Ireland or any part of Ireland would be far happier governed from London or Belfast or Timbuctoo. I never lose an opportunity myself to point out to my fellow-provincials in the Six Counties that their best interests would be served by throwing in their lot with their own fellow-countrymen, and that partition is a fatal policy for all of us.

But the secret Donegal petition was something very different from the mere advocacy of a political change by constitutional means. It contained the following demonstrably false allegations, tending 'to bring into hatred and contempt or to excite disaffection against' our 'government and constitution', and was, therefore, well within the Common Law definition of sedition:

(1) 'The confiscation of our property, and, perhaps, the taking of our lives are ever present possibilities'.

(2) 'Impartiality and fairness in the issue of cattle export licenses do not exist. Fianna Fáil supporters get all the licences they

require, whereas many loyal Protestants have been refused point blank'.

(3) 'Recently the Free State government have granted licences to their supporters to fish the waters of Lough Foyle, regardless of the rights of the owners of the fisheries'.

(4) 'Under the Free State Land Act of 1933 our title to our farms has been taken from us'.

You know the amount of pressure, social and otherwise, likely to be exercised in a country district to force individuals to take their stand with their fellows in a movement of this sort, and how hard it is for the average person in Ireland to refuse to act with his party or co-religionists. But it has now transpired that numbers of decent Protestants in the district, all or most of whom I feel sure would be Unionists in politics, absolutely refused to put their hands to a document containing so many scandalous falsehoods.[1]

Resolution from Raphoe District LOL no. 3, December 1937

We, the members of Raphoe District LOL no. 3, respectfully draw attention to the hardships created by the ban recently imposed upon milk entering Northern Ireland from the Irish Free State, and appeal to the members of the Northern Ireland cabinet to introduce an amending bill as early as possible.

To no one has this ban been more injurious than to the loyal farmers of east Donegal, many of whom are Orangemen and the very large majority Protestants. Owing to operations of the ban, one supplier has been already obliged to dispose of the services of three Orangemen, and many other producers will be obliged to follow suit. Where will these men find alternative employment? They will not receive it from the Free State government, and it is very unlikely that Roman Catholic farmers will offer them positions. If the ban remains, untold harm will be done to our illustrious Order in the Free State.

We would emphasize the fact that the Protestant community of Donegal are amongst the most loyal of any section in Ireland. This has been proved by experience. In 1914 thousands of Donegal men voluntarily answered the call of empire, and the battlefields of France and Flanders bear testimony to the sacrifices made by these sons of Ulster. A few years later, when the rebel south attempted to coerce Ulster into a republic for all Ireland, the stout-hearted Protestants of Donegal, at a cost of many lives and damage amounting to many thousands of pounds of property, stood shoulder to shoulder with their brethren from the North and, as their ancestors had done in 1688 and 1689, shouted those immortal words of 'No Surrender' in the faces of the forces of violence and disruption. Donegal loyalists will not readily forget the review by Lord Carson of the Ulster Volunteers in Raphoe in 1912, when thousands of Donegal men shouldered their arms to fight Ulster's battle, and nowhere was the Covenant signed more extensively than in east Donegal.

When attempts were made in 1920 to starve the loyal inhabitants of the *Maiden City* into submission, the east Donegal farmers were the first to come to their aid with supplies of milk, foodstuffs, farm produce and even home-made bread. When there was an effort to force an economic boycott upon Derry City the Donegal Loyalists were the first to rally to the support of the Protestant business houses of that city, which stands 'a maiden still'.

From recent legislation passed by the Free State parliament, it is apparent that the Free State government are doing all in their power to beggar the small Protestant community in the Free State. Several acts have been passed which are calculated to cause injury to this industrious and peace-loving community, and border operations have been intensified. It is useless to look for redress to the British government. Will it be said that the Northern government, for whose birth and existence we fought and bled, does not want us?

We appeal with all the vehemence at our disposal to our Orange brethren of the Six Counties to support us in our time of need; and having faith in the justice of our cause and confidence in the desire of our brethren to honour their obligations of brotherly love and loyalty, we know we will not appeal in vain.

In conclusion, we would point out that a large percentage of the producers now supplying milk in the districts formerly served by the Donegal vendors are Roman Catholics. Surely our Orange brethren in the Six Counties will not willingly see Free State Orangemen victimized to make way for Six-County Roman Catholic disloyalists?

Notes

ABBREVIATIONS

CDPRA	County Donegal Protestant Registration Association
IRA	Irish Republican Army
LOL	Loyal Orange Lodge
MBE	Member of the British Empire
MP	Member of Parliament
NAI	National Archives of Ireland
PRONI	Public Record Office of Northern Ireland
RUC	Royal Ulster Constabulary
TD	Teachta Dála
TNA	The National Archives (UK)
UK	United Kingdom
UUC	Ulster Unionist Council
UUP	Ulster Unionist Party
UVF	Ulster Volunteer Force
YMCA	Young Men's Christian Association

INTRODUCTION

1 PRONI, *Search the Ulster Covenant*: http://apps.proni.gov.uk/ulstercovenant/Search.aspx, accessed 30 Nov. 2021; PRONI, File containing lists of UVF Commanding Officers, D1327/4/20.

2 *Donegal Democrat*, 8 Nov. 2018; Paul Taylor, *Heroes or traitors? Experiences of southern Irish soldiers returning from the Great War, 1919–39* (Liverpool, 2015), pp 10–15.

3 Breandan Mac Giolla Choille (ed.), *Intelligence notes, 1913–16, preserved in the State Paper Office* (Dublin, 1966), p. 181.

4 Ibid., p. 205; PRONI, Total of men of military age [in Ireland] calculated [county by county] from appendix II, p. 23, D1507/A/20/32.

5 *Donegal Democrat*, 8 Nov. 2018.

6 Okan Ozseker, *Forging the border: Donegal and Derry in times of revolution, 1911–1940* (Newbridge, 2019), p. 99.

7 Irish Diplomatic Mission, *Irish councils for Irish freedom* (Washington, DC, 1920), p. 12.

8 PRONI, Letters of resignation of delegates from the Orange Order from counties Cavan, Donegal and Monaghan on the Ulster Unionist Council, D1327/18/28.

9 G.J. Hand, *Report of the Irish Boundary Commission, 1925* (Shannon, 1969), pp vii–xxii.

10 TNA, Summaries of cases in support of claims, CAB 61/159.

11 PRONI, Bundle of correspondence, D1327/18/27; Patrick Buckland, *Irish Unionism: the Anglo-Irish and the new Ireland, 1885–1922* (Dublin, 1973), p. 297.

12 TNA, Donegal County, Protestant Registration Association, CAB 61/51.

13 David Fitzpatrick, *Descendancy* (Cambridge, 2014), p. 57.

14 TNA, Report of the commission, CAB 61/161.

15 Hand, *Report of the Irish Boundary Commission, 1925*, p. xxii.

16 *Morning Post*, 7 Nov. 1925.

17 Department of Industry and Commerce, *Census of population, 1936, vol. iii* (Dublin, 1939), p. 19.

18 Patrick Buckland, *Irish Unionism, 1885–1923: a documentary history* (Belfast, 1973), p. 272.

19 Dennis Kennedy, *The widening gulf: Northern attitudes to the independent Irish state, 1919–49* (Belfast, 1988), pp 168–70; Uinseann MacEoin, *The IRA in the twilight years, 1923–1948* (Dublin, 1997), pp 311, 316.

20 Robin Bury, *Buried lives: the Protestants of southern Ireland* (Dublin, 2017), p. 169.

21 J.J. Tunney, 'From ascendancy to alienation: a study of Donegal's Protestant community, 1881–1932' (MA, University College Galway, 1985).

22 Fitzpatrick, *Descendancy*, pp 47–58; J.J. Tunney, 'The marquis, the reverend, the grand master and the major: Protestant politics in Donegal, 1863–1933' in William Nolan, Liam Ronayne and Máiread Dunleavy (eds), *Donegal, history and society: interdisciplinary essays on the history of an Irish county* (Dublin, 1995).

23 Brian Hughes and Conor Morrissey, *Southern Irish Loyalism, 1912–1949* (Liverpool, 2020).

24 Katherine Magee, 'Defying the partition of Ulster: Colonel John George Vaughan Hart and the Unionist experience of the Irish Revolution in east Donegal, c.1919–1944' in Brian Hughes and Conor Morrissey (eds), *Southern Irish Loyalism, 1912–1949* (Liverpool, 2022), pp 315–31.

25 John Bowman, *De Valera and the Ulster Question, 1917–1973* (Clarendon, 1983), p. 55.

26 Ian d'Alton and Ida Milne, *Protestant and Irish: the minority's search for place in independent Ireland* (Cork, 2019), p. 2.

27 Joseph Ruane and David Butler, 'Southern Irish Protestants: an example of de-ethnicisation?', *Nations and Nationalism*, 13:4 (Nov. 2007), pp 619–35.

29 Terence Dooley, *The plight of Monaghan Protestants, 1912–1926* (Dublin, 2000), p. 8.

29 Tim Wilson, *Frontiers of violence: conflict and identity in Ulster and Upper Silesia, 1918–1922* (Oxford, 2010).

1. ORIGINS OF THE MEMORIAL

1 Paul M. Canning, 'The impact of Eamon de Valera: domestic causes of the Anglo-Irish Economic War', *Albion*, 15:3 (Fall 1983), pp 179–205.

2 PRONI, Bundle of correspondence, memoranda, press, D989/A/8/2/63.

3 Ronan Fanning, *Éamon de Valera: a will to power* (London, 2015), pp 167–8.

4 PRONI, Irish Free State loyalists: correspondence, CAB/9/B/227/1.

5 B.M. Walker, *Parliamentary election results in Ireland, 1918–92: Irish elections to parliaments and parliamentary assemblies at Westminster, Belfast, Dublin, Strasbourg* (Dublin, 1992), pp 133, 139.

6 *Derry Journal*, 29 June 1934; *Londonderry Sentinel*, 28 June 1928.

7 Fitzpatrick, *Descendancy*, pp 47–58.

8 Dan Gawrecki, 'The determination of nationality in selected European countries up to 1938', *Prager wirtschafts- und sozialhistorische Mitteilungen – Prague Economic and Social History Papers*, 2:22 (2015), pp 27–54.

9 Dieter Nohlen and Phillip Stöver, *Elections in Europe: a data handbook* (Baden-Baden, 2010), p. 1510.

10 Walker, *Parliamentary election results in Ireland, 1918–92*, p. 139; *Londonderry Sentinel*, 28 June 1934.

11 *Donegal Democrat*, 16 July 1934.

12 *Derry Journal*, 28 Nov. 1934.

13 North Eastern Boundary Bureau, *Handbook of the Ulster question* (Dublin, 1923), pp 52, 68.

14 *Londonderry Sentinel*, 29 Nov. 1934.

15 *Londonderry Sentinel*, 14 July 1934.

16 Peter Leary, *Unapproved routes: histories of the Irish border, 1922–1972* (Oxford, 2016), p. 40.

17 NAI, Petition for the inclusion of Donegal in Northern Ireland, 2008/117/875.

18 *Belfast News-Letter*, 30 Mar. 1934.

19 NAI, Petition for the inclusion of Donegal in Northern Ireland, 2008/117/875.

20 *Belfast News-Letter*, 12 Nov. 1934; *Londonderry Sentinel*, 13 Nov. 1934.

21 NAI, Petition for the inclusion of Donegal in Northern Ireland, 2008/117/875; PRONI, Advisory Committee Minute Book, D2688/1/7.

22 NAI, Petition for the inclusion of Donegal in Northern Ireland, 2008/117/875.

23 Ibid.; *Derry Journal*, 12 Nov. 1934.

24 NAI, Petition for the inclusion of Donegal in Northern Ireland, 2008/117/875.

25 *Irish Independent*, 27 June 1942; *Wicklow People*, 15 July 1933; *Wicklow People*, 7 Oct. 1933.

26 NAI, Petition for the inclusion of Donegal in Northern Ireland, 2008/117/875.

27 Ibid.

28 TNA, Report of the commission, CAB 61/161; *Morning Post*, 7 Nov. 1925.

29 *Anglo-Celt*, 17 Nov. 1934; *Northern Standard*, 16 Nov. 1934; *Sligo Champion*, 12 Dec. 1934; *Offaly Independent*, 8 Dec. 1934; *Wicklow People*, 17 Nov. 1934; *Cork Examiner*, 12 Nov. 1934.

30 Dominic Bryan, *Orange parades: the politics of ritual, tradition and control* (London, 1999), p. 65.

31 NAI, Petition for the inclusion of Donegal in Northern Ireland, 2008/117/875.

32 Ibid.

33 Ibid.

34 Ibid.

35 *Londonderry Sentinel*, 16 Apr. 1946.

36 Ozseker, *Forging the border*, p. 189.

37 Richard English, 'Peadar O'Donnell: socialism and the republic, 1925–37', *Saothar*, 14 (1989), pp 47–58.

38 Magee, 'Defying the partition of Ulster'.

39 TNA, Report of the commission, CAB 61/161.

40 NAI, Petition for the inclusion of Donegal in Northern Ireland, 2008/117/875.

41 TNA, County Donegal Protestant Registration Association, CAB 61/51.

42 Donegal County Council, Donegal County Council minutes of meetings, 27 Nov. 1934, CC/1/1/21.

43 *Derry Journal*, 28 Nov. 1934.

44 Donegal County Council, Donegal County Council minutes of meetings, 27 Nov. 1934, CC/1/1/21.

45 *Derry Journal*, 28 Nov. 1934.

46 *Londonderry Sentinel*, 30 Nov. 1934.

47 *Derry Journal*, 12 Nov. 1934.

48 Buckland, *Irish Unionism: the Anglo-Irish and the new Ireland*, p. 297.

49 PRONI, Letters and papers of Lord Carson, D1507/A/49/1–50.

50 PRONI, Bundle of correspondence, memoranda, press, D989/A/8/2/63.

51 Patrick Buckland, *Ulster Unionism and origins of Northern Ireland, 1886–1922* (Dublin, 1973), p. 179.

52 North Eastern Boundary Bureau, *Handbook of the Ulster question*, pp 66–77.

53 PRONI, *Search the Ulster Covenant*: http://apps.proni.gov.uk/ulstercovenant/Search.aspx, accessed 30 Nov. 2021.

54 PRONI, Bundle of correspondence, memoranda, press, D989/A/8/2/63.

55 *Londonderry Sentinel*, 6 July 1905; 9 Mar. 1905.

56 TNA, Thomas Boyd Rankin, County Donegal, no. 1048, CO 762/66/5.

57 *Londonderry Sentinel*, 20 Apr. 1911; *Derry People & Donegal News*, 21 Feb. 1920.

58 *Fermanagh Herald*, 4 Sept. 1925.

59 NAI, Petition for the inclusion of Donegal in Northern Ireland, 2008/117/875.

60 *Derry Journal*, 20 Apr. 1919; *Fermanagh Herald*, 4 Sept. 1925.

61 *Belfast News-Letter*, 9 Jan. 1931.

62 *Strabane Chronicle*, 3 Dec. 1932; *Londonderry Sentinel*, 24 Apr. 1951; PRONI, Bundle of correspondence, D1327/18/27.

63 *Londonderry Sentinel*, 24 Apr. 1951.

64 *Londonderry Sentinel*, 1 July 1941.

65 *Strabane Chronicle*, 5 May 2005.

66 NAI, Trustees of Lifford Orange Lodge, Lifford, County Donegal, FIN/COMP/2/5/69.

67 Patrick Maume, 'Anti-Machiavel: three Ulster Nationalists of the age of de Valera', *Irish Political Studies*, 14:1 (1999), pp 43–63.

68 *Derry Journal*, 24 Oct. 1930.

69 *Londonderry Sentinel*, 13 July 1933; 29 Apr. 1930.

70 *Londonderry Sentinel*, 13 July 1935; 11 July 1931.

71 City of Derry Grand Orange Lodge, *Report of City Grand Lodge officers and district officers with private lodges, giving no., warrant, place and night of meeting, name and address of master and secretary of each lodge for 1936* (Londonderry, 1936), pp 7–11; the membership numbers for these east Donegal lodges were: Burt (LOL 1927) 40, Carrigans (LOL 1897) 60, Castlefin (LOL 774) unknown, Convoy (LOL 1005) 42, Lifford (LOL 1860) 60, Manorcunningham (LOL 1117) 60, Newtowncunningham (LOL 1063) 65,

Raphoe (LOL 1921) 50, St Johnston (LOL 992) 88, and Stranorlar (LOL 1061) 32.

72 *Derry People & Donegal News*, 17 Mar. 1951.

73 PRONI, Irish Free State Loyalists: correspondence, CAB/9/B/227/1.

74 PRONI, Milk supply in Northern Ireland, CAB/9/E/122/2; *Londonderry Sentinel*, 30 Jan. 1947.

75 PRONI, Bundle of correspondence, memoranda, press, D989/A/8/2/63.

76 Ibid.

77 Ibid.

78 PRONI, Irish Free State Loyalists: correspondence, CAB/9/B/227/1.

79 *Irish Times*, 6 Dec. 1934.

80 Grand Orange Lodge of Ireland, *Report of the proceedings at the general half-yearly meeting held in the Craig Memorial Orange Hall, Strabane, Co. Tyrone, on Wednesday, 13th day of June, 1934* (Belfast, 1934), pp 1–5.

81 *Londonderry Sentinel*, 14 June 1934.

82 *Derry Journal*, 15 June 1934.

83 *Londonderry Sentinel*, 15 Nov. 1934.

84 PRONI, Bundle of correspondence, memoranda, press, D989/A/8/2/63.

85 *Londonderry Sentinel*, 6 Nov. 1934.

86 *Derry Standard*, 7 Nov. 1934.

87 PRONI, Bundle of correspondence, memoranda, press, D989/A/8/2/63.

88 PRONI, Irish Free State Loyalists: correspondence, CAB/9/B/227/1.

89 *Derry Journal*, 14 Nov. 1934; *Derry Standard*, 14 Nov. 1934; *Irish Times*, 14 Nov. 1934; *Belfast News-Letter*, 15 Nov. 1934; *Londonderry Sentinel*, 15 Nov. 1934.

90 *Belfast News-Letter*, 12 Nov. 1934.

2. REACTIONS WITHIN THE BRITISH EMPIRE

1 *Queensland Times*, 17 Nov. 1934; *Auckland Star*, 24 Nov. 1934; *Natal Witness*, 17 Nov. 1934; *Bulawayo Chronicle*, 17 Nov. 1934.

2 Colonial Office (UK), *Annual Report of the Bechuanaland Protectorate* (London, 1950), p. 44; Northern Rhodesia government, *Northern Rhodesia: touring, fishing, hunting* (Lusaka, 1938), p. 66; Union of South Africa Government Information Office, *South Africa-American Survey*, vol. 1 (New York, 1947), p. 16.

3 *Sentinel and Orange and Protestant Advocate*, 5 Jan. 1933.

4 Irish Loyalist Imperial Federation, 'Donegal Loyalists Petition', *Notes From Ireland*, 32:3 (May 1935), p. 29.

5 Irish Loyalist Imperial Federation, *Notes From Ireland*, 32:2 (Nov. 1934).

6 *New York Times*, 22 Apr. 1921.

7 *New York Times*, 5 Dec. 1934; 29 Nov. 1934.

8 *New York Times*, 15 Nov. 1934.

9 *Evening Telegram*, 17 Nov. 1934.

10 Robert Cole, *Propaganda, censorship and Irish neutrality in the Second World War* (Edinburgh, 2006), pp 26–51.

11 Francine McKenzie, '"The last-ditch defender of national sovereignty at Geneva": the realities behind Canadian diplomacy during the Ethiopian crisis', *Collision of empires: Italy's invasion of Ethiopia and its international impact* (London, 2016), pp 177–87.

12 Gene Allen, *Making national news: a history of Canadian press* (Toronto, 2014), p. 3.

13 Robert McLaughlin, *Irish Canadian conflict and the struggle for Irish independence, 1912–1925* (Toronto, 2013), pp 26–65.

14 *Derry Journal*, 16 Nov. 1934; *Irish Times*, 6 Dec. 1934; *Daily Express*, 14 Nov. 1934.

15 *Derry Journal*, 16 Nov. 1934.

16 NAI, Petition for the inclusion of Donegal in Northern Ireland, 2008/117/875.

17 *Derry Weekly News*, 17 Nov. 1934; *Donegal Vindicator*, 17 Nov. 1934.

18 *Donegal Democrat*, 17 Nov. 1934; *Derry People & Tirconaill News*, 17 Nov. 1934.

19 *Derry Journal*, 12 Nov. 1934.

20 *Londonderry Sentinel*, 13 Nov. 1934.

21 *Derry Journal*, 14 Nov. 1934.

22 NAI, Petition for the inclusion of Donegal in Northern Ireland, 2008/117/875.

23 *Derry Journal*, 16 Nov. 1934; *Londonderry Sentinel*, 13 Nov. 1934.

24 NAI, Petition for the inclusion of Donegal in Northern Ireland, 2008/117/875.

25 PRONI, Irish Free State Loyalists: correspondence, CAB/9/B/227/1.

26 *Irish Independent*, 16 Nov. 1934.

27 NAI, Petition for the inclusion of Donegal in Northern Ireland, 2008/117/875.

28 Cormac Moore, *Birth of the border: the impact of partition in Ireland* (Newbridge, 2019), p. 201.

29 *Belfast News-Letter*, 16 Nov. 1934.

30 Guy Beiner, *Forgetful remembrance: social forgetting and vernacular historiography of a rebellion in Ulster* (Oxford, 2018), p. 437; Ozseker, *Forging the border*, p. 99.

31 Leary, *Unapproved routes*, p. 68.

32 NAI, Petition for the inclusion of Donegal in Northern Ireland, 2008/117/875.

33 PRONI, Irish Free State loyalists: correspondence, CAB/9/B/227/1.

34 *Irish Times*, 6 Dec. 1934.

35 *Northern Whig and Belfast Post*, 21 Nov. 1934.

36 *Londonderry Sentinel*, 15 Nov. 1934; 1 Jan. 1934; *Strabane Weekly News*, 24 Nov. 1934.

37 *Belfast News-Letter*, 3 June 1924; *Londonderry Sentinel*, 24 Nov. 1934; *Belfast News-Letter*, 23 Nov. 1934.

38 *Belfast News-Letter*, 16 Jan. 1925.

39 *Belfast News-Letter*, 23 Nov. 1934.

40 *Irish Independent*, 23 Nov. 1934.

41 *Belfast News-Letter*, 23 Nov. 1934.

42 *Londonderry Sentinel*, 24 Nov. 1934.

43 *Ballymena Weekly Telegraph*, 24 Nov. 1934.

44 *Northern Whig and Belfast Post*, 19 Nov. 1934.

45 Ibid.

46 *Belfast Telegraph*, 19 Nov. 1934.

47 *Belfast Newsletter*, 4 Dec. 1934.

48 Ibid.

49 Houses of the Oireachtas debates, *Dáil Éireann debate – Thursday 6 Dec. 1934: Ceisteanna – Questions. Oral Answers. – District Justice's Statement*, www.oireachtas.ie/en/debates/debate/dail/1934-12-06/3/?highlight%5B0%5D=major&highlight%5B1%5D=myles&highlight%5B2%5D=walsh, accessed 27 May 2019.

50 *Daily Telegraph*, 16 Nov. 1934.

51 *Irish Independent*, 16 Nov. 1934; *Connaught Telegraph*, 24 Nov. 1934.

52 *Kerry Reporter*, 8 Dec. 1934; *The Liberator*, 6 Dec. 1934; *Donegal Vindicator*, 15 Dec. 1934.

53 *Connaught Telegraph*, 15 Dec. 1934.

54 *Evening Herald*, 6 Dec. 1934.

55 *The Sun*, 16 Nov. 1934; *Daily Standard*, 16 Nov. 1934.

56 Ashley Jackson, *The British Empire and the First World War* (Abingdon, 2016), pp 1–15.

57 Kent Fedorowich, 'Reconstruction and resettlement: the politicization of Irish migration to Australia and Canada, 1919–29', *English Historical Review*, 114:459 (Nov. 1999), pp 1143–78.

58 *Natal Mercury*, 17 Nov. 1934.

59 *Belfast News-Letter*, 23 Nov. 1934.

60 *Daily Telegraph*, 17 Nov. 1934; *Bulawayo Chronicle*, 17 Nov. 1934; *Cape Argus*, 16 Nov. 1934.

61 PRONI, Bundle of correspondence, memoranda, press, D989/A/8/2/63.

62 J.W. McAuley and Paul Nesbitt-Larking, *Contemporary Orangeism in Canada: identity, Nationalism and religion* (Basingstoke, 2017), pp 63–83; Brad Patterson, *Ulster–New Zealand migration and cultural transfers* (Dublin, 2006), p. 156.

63 W.J. Smyth, *Toronto, the Belfast of Canada: the Orange Order and the shaping of municipal culture* (Toronto, 2015), pp 20–7; Mark Sheftall, 'Mythologising the dominion fighting man: Australian and Canadian narratives of the First World War soldier, 1914–39', *Australian Historical Studies*, 46:1 (Feb. 2015), pp 81–99.

64 Robert McLaughlin, *Irish Canadian conflict and the struggle for Irish independence, 1912–1925* (Toronto, 2011), p. 47.

65 *Irish Times*, 21 Nov. 1934.

66 *Londonderry Sentinel*, 22 Nov. 1934; *Derry Journal*, 23 Nov. 1934; *Strabane Weekly News*, 24 Nov. 1934.

67 NAI, Petition for the inclusion of Donegal in Northern Ireland, 2008/117/875.

3. RESPONSES OF THE BRITISH AND NORTHERN IRISH GOVERNMENTS

1 Northern Ireland House of Commons, *The parliamentary debates: official report, vol. XVII: second session of the fourth parliament of Northern Ireland, 25 & 26 year of the reign of his majesty King George V. House of Commons. Session 1934–1935* (Belfast, 1935), p. 458.

2 Ibid.

3 Ibid.

4 Eamon Phoenix, 'Healy, Cahir', *Dictionary of Irish biography*, vol. 4

(Cambridge, 2009), pp 555–8; Marie Coleman, 'Little, Patrick John ('P.J.')', *Dictionary of Irish biography*, vol. 5 (Cambridge, 2009), pp 517–19.

5 PRONI, Letter from F.J. Little, 28 Rathgar Road, Dublin, to Healy, 20 Nov. 1934, D2991/A/3/73.

6 PRONI, Copy reply from Healy, Enniskillen, to F.J. Little, 28 Rathgar Road, Dublin, 2 Dec. 1934, D2991/A/3/14.

7 Northern Ireland House of Commons, *Parliamentary debates: session 1934–1935*, p. 459.

8 Ibid.

9 *Belfast News-Letter*, 10 Dec. 1934.

10 *Irish Times*, 10 Dec. 1934; *Daily Express*, 10 Dec. 1934.

11 PRONI, File of minutes of the Refugee Committee, D1327/15/6.

12 A.F. Parkinson, *Belfast's unholy war: the troubles of the 1920s* (Dublin, 2004), p. 110.

13 PRONI, Correspondence regarding the Loyalist Relief Fund, D1327/14/6/33.

14 Paul McMahon, *British spies and Irish rebels: British intelligence and Ireland, 1916–1945* (Woodbridge, 2008), p. 188.

15 *Belfast News-Letter*, 14 Jan. 1935.

16 *Belfast News-Letter*, 10 Dec. 1934; *Londonderry Sentinel*, 8 Dec. 1934.

17 Andy Bielenberg, 'Exodus: the emigration of southern Irish Protestants during the Irish War of Independence and the Civil War', *Past & Present*, 218:1 (Feb. 2013), pp 199–233.

18 *Londonderry Sentinel*, 18 Dec. 1934.

19 *Belfast News-Letter*, 14 Jan. 1935.

20 Geoffrey Warner, 'Putting pressure on O'Neill', *Irish Studies Review*, 13:1 (Jan. 2005), pp 13–31.

21 *Irish Times*, 8 Dec. 1934.

22 *Northern Whig and Belfast Post*, 24 Dec. 1934; *Irish Weekly and Ulster Examiner*, 15 Dec. 1934.

23 NAI, Petition for the inclusion of Donegal in Northern Ireland, 2008/117/875.

24 PRONI, Modern Ireland: cabinet papers of the Stormont administration, 1921–1972, CAB/4/336.

25 NAI, Petition for the inclusion of Donegal in Northern Ireland, 2008/117/875.

26 *Londonderry Sentinel*, 26 Feb. 1935.

27 NAI, Petition for the inclusion of Donegal in Northern Ireland, 2008/117/875.

28 *Belfast Telegraph*, 19 Nov. 1934.

29 *Derry Journal*, 7 Jan. 1935.

30 *Derry Journal*, 4 Mar. 1935.

31 *Belfast Telegraph*, 8 May 1935.

32 *Londonderry Sentinel*, 7 May 1935; *Derry Journal*, 8 May 1935; *Londonderry Sentinel*, 11 May 1935.

33 *Irish Independent*, 7 May 1935; *Yorkshire Post*, 7 May 1935; *Nottingham Journal*, 7 May 1935.

34 *Derry Journal*, 15 July 1935.

35 *Belfast News-Letter*, 17 July 1935.

36 *Ulster Herald*, 20 July 1935.

37 *Evening Herald*, 29 July 1935.

38 *Belfast News-Letter*, 26 July 1935; *Northern Standard*, 26 July 1935.

39 *Belfast News-Letter*, 25 July 1935.

40 *Londonderry Sentinel*, 23 Mar. 1935.

41 *Derry Journal*, 2 Jan. 1935.

42 *Derry Journal*, 11 Oct. 1935.

43 NAI, Petition for the inclusion of Donegal in Northern Ireland, 2008/117/875.

44 *Derry Journal*, 11 Oct. 1935.

45 NAI, Petition for the inclusion of Donegal in Northern Ireland, 2008/117/875.

4. DERRY-DONEGAL MILK WAR

1 *Belfast News-Letter*, 17 Dec. 1934.

2 PRONI, Milk supply in Northern Ireland, CAB/9/E/122/2.

3 *Strabane Chronicle*, 19 Jan. 1935.

4 Ibid.

5 *Belfast News-Letter*, 10 Jan. 1935.

6 *Irish Independent*, 3 Jan. 1935.

7 *Belfast News-Letter*, 10 Jan. 1935.

8 *Belfast News-Letter*, 11 Jan. 1935.

9 *Irish Examiner*, 15 Jan. 1935.

10 *Irish Independent*, 5 Jan. 1935.

11 *Donegal Democrat*, 12 Jan. 1935; *Belfast News-Letter*, 15 Jan. 1935; *Irish Independent*, 5 Jan. 1935.

12 NAI, Petition for the inclusion of Donegal in Northern Ireland, 2008/117/875.

13 *Belfast News-Letter*, 19 Jan. 1935.

14 *Derry Journal*, 1 July 1936.

15 *Londonderry Sentinel*, 4 July 1936.

16 *Belfast News-Letter*, 17 Sept. 1937.

17 *Londonderry Sentinel*, 23 Dec. 1937.

18 *Irish Independent*, 18 Aug. 1939.
19 *Irish Independent*, 7 Feb. 1940; *Strabane Chronicle*, 16 Nov. 1940.
20 *Derry People & Donegal News*, 4 Dec. 1937; *Londonderry Sentinel*, 14 June 1938.
21 Grand Orange Lodge of Ireland, *Report of the proceedings at the general half-yearly meeting held in the Orange Hall, Sandy Row, Belfast, on Wednesday, 8th December 1937* (Belfast, 1938), pp 25–6.
22 *Londonderry Sentinel*, 9 June 1938.

CONCLUSION

1 Wilson, *Frontiers of violence*, pp 27–35.
2 Harpo, 'Liberate Donegal petition', *GoPetition*: www.gopetition.com/petitions/liberate-donegal.html, accessed 1 Jan. 2019.
3 Orin Mhando, 'Launch a referendum for the Republic of Ireland on whether or not to rejoin the United Kingdom in 2020', *Change.org*: www.change.org/p/house-of-the-oireachtas-michael-d-higgins-seanad-%C3%A9ireann-launch-a-referendum-for-the-republic-of-ireland-to-rejoin-the-united-kingdom-in-2020, accessed 13 July 2015.
4 The Oireachtas, *Online Petitions – oireachtas petition*: http://petitions.oireachtas.ie/online_petitions.nsf/Published_Petitions_EN/F79C7094A87D5C8280257EFA0043592D?opendocument&type=published+petition&lang=EN&r=0.99311818112459, accessed 3 July 2019.
5 UK Government and Parliament, 'Invite Co. Donegal to re-join the United Kingdom', *Petitions*: https://petition.parliament.uk/archived/petitions/114068, accessed 31 Dec. 2021.
6 *Derry Journal*, 6 Jan. 1978.
7 K.R. Dodds, *The demons of discord* (Bloomington, 2014), pp 248–70.
8 Ulster-Scots Community Network, *County Donegal & the Plantation of Ulster* (Belfast, 2013), p. 38.

APPENDIX 5

1 *Irish Times*, 21 Nov. 1934.